pasta

HOMESTYLE

pasta

MURDOCH BOOKS

contents

The wonderful world of pasta

Italy is famous for its passion and style, so it's a little disappointing to discover that the Italian word 'pasta' just means 'paste'. 'Paste' hardly does justice to the astonishing diversity of pasta. Yet in its simplest form, pasta is nothing more than flour and water, with more elaborate types including egg yolk for richness, vegetable juices for colour or even certain spices or herbs for extra flavour.

Pasta comes in dried or fresh form and in an extraordinary variety of shapes and sizes. These range from cute bow-ties (farfalle), stubby tubes (penne), tiny rice shapes (risoni) and long, graceful strands (linguine, fettuccine or spaghetti, to name but a few) to large, broad sheets (lasagne).

Pasta can form the basis of a thick, nourishing soup. Minestrone is a classic; but other delicious possibilities are bean soup with sausage and pasta, or ratatouille and pasta soup. Pasta can make for simple, unfussy eating, paired with easy combinations such as spinach and bacon, peas and prosciutto or rocket and mushrooms, or even just some garlic, parsley and a squeeze of lemon. Pasta dishes are often hearty, sauced with long-simmered concoctions such as the timeless, meaty bolognese or a healthy lentil sauce. They can be simple and elegant (angel hair with creamy garlic prawns, for example), or utterly rustic, evoking the earthy traditions of the Italian countryside, thanks to sauces such as pesto, marinara or puttanesca. Sometimes pasta is formed into little, stuffed parcels (think of ravioli, tortellini or agnolotti), making dishes that are always satisfying, both in the cooking and in the eating. At other times pasta is decidedly light and fresh, especially when paired with seafood or used as the basis for a summery salad or frittata.

Pasta suits any and every season, occasion, budget and schedule—the toughest part is deciding which shape and sauce to choose. *Homestyle Pasta* makes that part easier, assembling in one book more delicious pasta possibilities than you could dream of. The only thing it can't do is cook them for you; and where would be the fun in that, anyway? Buon appetito!

Classic sauces

Spaghetti vongole

PREPARATION TIME: 25 MINUTES + OVERNIGHT SOAKING | TOTAL COOKING TIME: 35 MINUTES | SERVES 4

1 kg (2 lb 4 oz) small fresh clams (vongole) in shells, cleaned (see NOTE) or 750 g (1 lb 10 oz) tinned clams in brine
1 tablespoon lemon juice
4 tablespoons olive oil
3 garlic cloves, crushed
850 g (1 lb 14 oz) tinned chopped tomatoes
250 g (9 oz) spaghetti
4 tablespoons chopped parsley

1 Place the cleaned clams in a large saucepan with the lemon juice. Cover the pan tightly and shake over medium heat for 7–8 minutes until the shells open (discard any clams that do not open in this time). Remove the clams from their shells. If using tinned clams, rinse well, drain and set aside.

2 Heat the oil in a large saucepan. Add the garlic and cook over low heat for 5 minutes. Add the tomatoes and stir well. Bring to the boil and simmer, covered, for 20 minutes. Add the clams to the sauce and season with freshly ground black pepper. Stir until heated through.

3 Meanwhile, cook the pasta in a large saucepan of rapidly boiling salted water until *al dente*. Drain well and return to the pan. Add the sauce and chopped parsley and toss gently.

NOTE: *To clean the clams, any sand and grit needs to be drawn out of the shells. Combine 2 tablespoons each of salt and plain flour with enough water to make a paste. Add to a large bucket or bowl of cold water and soak the clams in this mixture overnight. Drain and scrub the shells well, then rinse thoroughly and drain again.*

NUTRITION PER SERVE
Protein 35 g; Fat 25 g; Carbohydrate 55 g; Dietary Fibre 7 g; Cholesterol 355 mg; 2420 kJ (580 Cal)

If using tinned clams, rinse them thoroughly and then drain well.

Add the clams to the sauce and season with freshly ground black pepper.

Add the clam sauce and the parsley to the warm pasta in the saucepan and toss gently.

Pasta with gorgonzola sauce

PREPARATION TIME: 10 MINUTES | TOTAL COOKING TIME: 15 MINUTES | SERVES 4–6

375 g (13 oz) spaghetti or bucatini
200 g (7 oz) gorgonzola cheese (see NOTE)
250 g (9 oz/1 cup) fresh ricotta cheese
1 tablespoon salted butter
1 celery stalk, finely chopped
300 ml (10½ fl oz) pouring (whipping) cream

1 Cook the pasta in a large saucepan of rapidly boiling salted water until *al dente*. Drain well and return to the pan to keep warm. Meanwhile, chop the gorgonzola into small cubes and beat the ricotta until it is smooth.

2 Heat the butter in a frying pan, add the celery and stir for 2 minutes. Add the cream, ricotta and gorgonzola and season to taste.

3 Bring to the boil over low heat, stirring constantly. Reduce the heat and simmer for 1 minute. Toss well with the pasta.

NOTE: *Gorgonzola is a rich strong Italian blue-veined cheese.*

NUTRITION PER SERVE (6)
Protein 20 g; Fat 40 g; Carbohydrate 46 g; Dietary Fibre 3 g; Cholesterol 126 mg; 2614 kJ (624 Cal)

While the pasta is cooking, chop the gorgonzola cheese into cubes.

Cook the celery for 2 minutes before adding the cream, ricotta and gorgonzola.

Bring the sauce to the boil over low heat, stirring constantly to thicken it.

Pasta pomodoro

PREPARATION TIME: 15 MINUTES I TOTAL COOKING TIME: 15 MINUTES I SERVES 4

500 g (1 lb 2 oz) pasta (see NOTE)
1½ tablespoons olive oil
1 onion, very finely chopped
800 g (1 lb 12 oz) tinned chopped tomatoes
small handful basil leaves

1 Cook the pasta in a large saucepan of rapidly boiling salted water until *al dente*. Drain well and return to the pan to keep warm.

2 Heat the oil in a large frying pan. Add the onion and cook over medium heat until softened. Stir in the tomato and simmer for 5–6 minutes, or until the sauce has reduced slightly and thickened. Season to taste. Stir in the basil leaves and cook for another minute. Gently toss through the pasta and serve immediately.

NOTE: *Traditionally, pomodoro is served with tagliatelle. It is shown here with penne.*

NUTRITION PER SERVE
Protein 20 g; Fat 10 g; Carbohydrate 95 g; Dietary Fibre 10 g; Cholesterol 5 mg; 2295 kJ (545 Cal)

To finely chop an onion, cut it in half, then thinly slice, without cutting all the way through.

Then slice finely in one direction and then the opposite, to make fine cubes.

Pasta bolognese

PREPARATION TIME: 25 MINUTES | TOTAL COOKING TIME: 2½ HOURS | SERVES 4

50 g (1¾ oz) salted butter
180 g (6¼ oz) thick bacon slices or speck,
    finely chopped
1 large onion, finely chopped
1 carrot, finely chopped
1 celery stalk, finely chopped
400 g (14 oz) lean minced (ground) beef
670 ml (23 fl oz/2⅔ cups) beef stock
250 g (9 oz) tinned chopped tomatoes
125 ml (4 fl oz/½ cup) dry red wine
¼ teaspoon freshly grated nutmeg
500 g (1 lb 2 oz) pasta (see NOTE)
grated parmesan cheese, for serving

NUTRITION PER SERVE
Protein 45 g; Fat 35 g; Carbohydrate 95 g; Dietary
Fibre 9 g; Cholesterol 145 mg; 3860 kJ (920 Cal)

1 Heat half the butter in a heavy-based frying pan. Add the bacon and cook until golden. Add the onion, carrot and celery and cook over low heat for 8 minutes, stirring often.

2 Increase the heat, add the remaining butter and, when the pan is hot, add the beef. Break up any lumps with a wooden spoon and stir until brown. Add the beef stock, tomato, wine, nutmeg and season to taste.

3 Bring to the boil and then reduce the heat and simmer, covered, over very low heat for 2–5 hours, adding more stock if the sauce becomes too dry. The longer the sauce is cooked, the more flavour it will have.

4 Cook the pasta in a large saucepan of rapidly boiling salted water until *al dente*. Drain well and serve with the sauce and freshly grated parmesan cheese.

NOTE: *Traditionally, bolognese is served with tagliatelle.*

Finely chop the thick bacon slices or speck, after removing any rind.

Use the finest cutting side of the grater for the whole nutmeg.

Pasta primavera

PREPARATION TIME: 25 MINUTES | TOTAL COOKING TIME: 20 MINUTES | SERVES 4

500 g (1 lb 2 oz) pasta (see NOTE)
155 g (5½ oz/1 cup) frozen broad (fava) beans
200 g (7 oz) sugar snap peas
150 g (5½ oz) asparagus spears
30 g (1 oz) salted butter
250 ml (9 fl oz/1 cup) pouring (whipping) cream
60 g (2¼ oz) grated parmesan cheese

1 Cook the pasta in a large saucepan of rapidly boiling salted water until *al dente*. Drain well and return to the pan to keep warm.

2 Cook the beans in boiling water for 2 minutes, then refresh in iced water and drain. Remove the skins from the beans—you can usually just squeeze them out, otherwise carefully slit the skins first.

3 Trim the stalks from the peas and snap the tough woody ends from the asparagus spears. Cut the asparagus into short lengths.

4 Melt the butter in a frying pan. Add the vegetables, cream and parmesan cheese. Simmer gently for 3–4 minutes, or until the peas and asparagus are just tender. Season to taste. Pour the sauce over the warm pasta and toss gently. Serve immediately.

NOTE: *Traditionally, primavera sauce is served with spaghetti. We have shown it with farfalle.*

If the broad beans will not slip out of their skins easily, gently slit or break the ends first.

Trim the stalks from the sugar snap peas. Snap the woody ends from the asparagus.

NUTRITION PER SERVE
Protein 30 g; Fat 35 g; Carbohydrate 95 g; Dietary Fibre 12 g; Cholesterol 105 mg; 3420 kJ (815 Cal)

Pasta boscaiola

PREPARATION TIME: 15 MINUTES | TOTAL COOKING TIME: 25 MINUTES | SERVES 4

500 g (1 lb 2 oz) pasta (see NOTE)
1 tablespoon olive oil
6 bacon slices, chopped
200 g (7 oz) button mushrooms, sliced
625 ml (21½ fl oz/2½ cups) pouring
   (whipping) cream
2 spring onions (scallions), sliced
1 tablespoon chopped parsley

1 Cook the pasta in a large saucepan of rapidly boiling salted water until *al dente*. Drain well and return to the pan to keep warm.

2 Meanwhile, heat the oil in a large frying pan, add the bacon and mushrooms and cook, stirring, for 5 minutes, or until golden brown.

3 Add a little of the cream and stir well with a wooden spoon.

4 Add the remaining cream, bring to the boil and cook over high heat for 15 minutes, or until thick enough to coat the back of a spoon. Add the spring onion. Pour the sauce over the pasta and toss well. Serve sprinkled with the parsley.

NOTE: *This sauce is normally served with spaghetti, but you can use any pasta. We have shown it with casarecce. If you are short on time and don't have 15 minutes to reduce the sauce, it can be thickened with 2 teaspoons of cornflour (cornstarch) mixed with 1 tablespoon of water. Stir until the mixture boils and thickens. 'Boscaiola' means woodcutter—collecting mushrooms is part of the woodcutter heritage.*

Add a little of the cream and scrape the bottom of the pan with a wooden spoon.

Cook the sauce over high heat until it is thick enough to coat the back of a wooden spoon.

NUTRITION PER SERVE
Protein 30 g; Fat 60 g; Carbohydrate 95 g; Dietary Fibre 8 g; Cholesterol 200 mg; 4310 kJ (1025 Cal)

Pasta marinara

PREPARATION TIME: 50 MINUTES | TOTAL COOKING TIME: 30 MINUTES | SERVES 4

1 tablespoon olive oil

1 onion, chopped

2 garlic cloves, crushed

125 ml (4 fl oz/½ cup) dry red wine

2 tablespoons tomato paste (concentrated pureé)

425 g (15 oz) tinned chopped tomatoes

250 ml (9 fl oz/1 cup) bottled tomato pasta sauce

1 tablespoon chopped basil

1 tablespoon chopped oregano

12 mussels, scrubbed and beards removed (discard any which are open and don't close if tapped)

30 g (1 oz) salted butter

125 g (4½ oz) small squid tubes, sliced

125 g (4½ oz) boneless white fish fillets, cubed

200 g (7 oz) raw prawns (shrimp), peeled and deveined, tails intact

500 g (1 lb 2 oz) pasta

1 Heat the olive oil in a large saucepan. Add the onion and garlic and cook over low heat for 2–3 minutes. Increase the heat to medium and add the wine, tomato paste, tomato and pasta sauce. Simmer, stirring occasionally, for 5–10 minutes or until the sauce thickens slightly. Stir in the fresh herbs and season. Keep warm.

2 Heat 125 ml (4 fl oz/½ cup) water in a saucepan. Add the mussels, cover the pan tightly and steam for 3–5 minutes, or until the mussels have opened. Discard any that don't open in this time. Set the mussels aside and stir the cooking liquid into the tomato sauce.

3 Heat the butter in a frying pan and sauté the squid, fish and prawns, in batches, for 1–2 minutes, or until cooked. Add the seafood, including the mussels, to the warm tomato sauce and stir gently.

4 Cook the pasta in a large saucepan of rapidly boiling salted water until *al dente*. Drain well and toss gently with the seafood sauce.

NUTRITION PER SERVE
Protein 40 g; Fat 10 g; Carbohydrate 100 g; Dietary Fibre 10 g; Cholesterol 205 mg; 2840 kJ (675 Cal)

Scrub the mussels and pull away their beards. Discard any open mussels.

Remove the quills from inside the squid tubes and slice the tubes into thin rings.

Pasta with pesto

PREPARATION TIME: 10–15 MINUTES | TOTAL COOKING TIME: 15 MINUTES | SERVES 4–6

500 g (1 lb 2 oz) pasta (see NOTE)
3 tablespoons pine nuts
2 very large handfuls basil leaves
2 garlic cloves, peeled
½ teaspoon salt
3 tablespoons grated parmesan cheese
2 tablespoons grated pecorino cheese, optional
125 ml (4 fl oz/½ cup) olive oil

1 Cook the pasta in a large saucepan of rapidly boiling salted water until *al dente*. Drain well and return to the pan to keep warm.

2 Meanwhile, toast the pine nuts in a dry heavy-based frying pan over low heat for 2–3 minutes, or until golden. Allow to cool. Process the pine nuts, basil leaves, garlic, salt and parmesan and pecorino (if using) cheeses in a food processor for 20 seconds, or until finely chopped.

3 With the motor running, gradually add the oil in a thin steady stream until a paste is formed. Add freshly ground black pepper, to taste. Toss the sauce with the warm pasta until the pasta is well coated.

NOTE: *Traditionally, linguine is used with pesto but you can serve it with any pasta of your choice. Pesto sauce can be made up to 1 week in advance and refrigerated in an airtight container. Ensure the pesto is tightly packed and seal the surface with some plastic wrap or pour a little extra oil over the top to prevent the pesto turning black. Each time you use the pesto reseal the surface with a little oil.*

Process the pine nuts, basil leaves, garlic, salt and cheeses for about 20 seconds.

With the motor running, add the olive oil in a thin steady stream, until a paste is formed.

NUTRITION PER SERVE (6)
Protein 15 g; Fat 30 g; Carbohydrate 60 g; Dietary Fibre 5 g; Cholesterol 8 mg; 2280 kJ (540 Cal)

Pasta amatriciana

PREPARATION TIME: 25 MINUTES I TOTAL COOKING TIME: 20 MINUTES I SERVES 4–6

6 thin slices pancetta or 3 bacon slices
1 kg (2 lb 4 oz) very ripe tomatoes
500 g (1 lb 2 oz) pasta (see NOTES)
1 tablespoon olive oil
1 small onion, very finely chopped
2 teaspoons very finely chopped fresh chilli
    (see NOTES)
parmesan cheese shaved, for serving

1   Finely chop the pancetta or bacon. Score a cross in the base of each tomato. Soak in boiling water for 1 minute, then drain and plunge into cold water briefly. Peel the skin away from the cross. Halve the tomatoes, remove the seeds and chop the flesh.

2   Cook the pasta in a large saucepan of rapidly boiling salted water until *al dente*. Drain well and return to the pan to keep warm.

3   Meanwhile, heat the oil in a heavy-based frying pan. Add the pancetta or bacon, onion and chilli and stir over medium heat for 3 minutes. Add the tomato and season to taste. Reduce the heat and simmer for 3 minutes. Add the sauce to the pasta and toss until well combined. Serve garnished with shavings of parmesan cheese, if desired.

NOTES: *It is believed this dish originated in the town of Amatrice, where bacon is a prized local product. For a change from ordinary tomatoes, you can try roma (plum) tomatoes in this recipe. They are firm-fleshed with few seeds and have a rich flavour when cooked. Traditionally, bucatini is served with this sauce, but you can use any pasta you prefer. It is shown here with penne.*

To avoid skin irritation, wear rubber gloves when chopping or seeding chillies.

NUTRITION PER SERVE (6)
Protein 15 g; Fat 9 g; Carbohydrate 60 g; Dietary Fibre 6 g; Cholesterol 15 mg; 1640 kJ (390 Cal)

Remove the tomatoes from the cold water and peel the skin down from the cross.

Halve the tomatoes and scrape out the seeds with a teaspoon.

Pasta ragù

PREPARATION TIME: 25 MINUTES | TOTAL COOKING TIME: 2½ HOURS | SERVES 4–6

180 g (6¼ oz) speck, or thick bacon slices
150 g (5½ oz) chicken livers
60 g (2¼ oz/¼ cup) salted butter
1 large onion, finely chopped
1 carrot, finely chopped
1 celery stalk, finely chopped
200 g (7 oz) minced (ground) veal
200 g (7 oz) minced (ground) pork
500 ml (17 fl oz/2 cups) beef stock
250 g (9 oz) tinned chopped tomatoes
125 ml (4 fl oz/½ cup) dry red wine
¼ teaspoon grated nutmeg
500 g (1 lb 2 oz) pasta
grated parmesan cheese, for serving

NUTRITION PER SERVE (6)
Protein 38 g; Fat 25 g; Carbohydrate 62 g; Dietary
Fibre 5 g; Cholesterol 207 mg; 2644 kJ (632 Cal)

1   Chop the speck (or bacon) finely. Slice and finely chop the chicken livers. Heat about half the butter in a heavy-based frying pan. Add the speck and cook until golden brown. Add the onion, carrot and celery and cook over low heat for about 8 minutes, stirring occasionally.

2   Increase the heat, add the remaining butter and, when the pan is quite hot, add the veal and pork. Break up any lumps with a fork and stir until brown. Add the livers and cook, stirring, until they change colour. Add the stock, tomato, wine and nutmeg. Season, bring to the boil and simmer, covered, over very low heat for 2–5 hours, adding a little more stock if the sauce becomes too dry. The longer you cook the sauce the more flavour it will have.

3   Cook the pasta in a large saucepan of rapidly boiling salted water until *al dente*. Drain well and return to the pan. Add half the sauce and toss to combine. Serve the rest of the sauce over the top, with grated parmesan cheese.

VARIATION: *For a creamier sauce, you can add 200 ml (7 fl oz) pouring (whipping) cream just before serving.*

Use a large sharp knife to finely chop the speck or bacon.

Slice the chicken livers, then chop them finely and set aside.

Break up any lumps of mince with a fork and stir until brown.

Pasta napolitana

PREPARATION TIME: 20 MINUTES I TOTAL COOKING TIME: 1 HOUR I SERVES 4–6

2 tablespoons olive oil
1 onion, finely chopped
1 carrot, finely chopped
1 celery stalk, finely chopped
500 g (1 lb 2 oz) very ripe tomatoes, chopped
2 tablespoons chopped parsley
2 teaspoons sugar
500 g (1 lb 2 oz) pasta (see NOTE)

1 Heat the oil in a heavy-based saucepan. Add the onion, carrot and celery. Cover and cook for 10 minutes over low heat, stirring occasionally.

2 Add the tomato to the pan with the parsley, sugar and 125 ml (4 fl oz/½ cup) water. Bring to the boil, reduce the heat to low, cover and simmer for 45 minutes, stirring occasionally. Season to taste. If necessary, add up to 185 ml (6 fl oz/¾ cup) more water if the sauce needs thinning.

3 Cook the pasta in a large saucepan of rapidly boiling salted water until *al dente*. Drain well and return to the pan. Toss gently with the sauce.

NOTE: *Traditionally, spaghetti is served with this sauce but we have shown fusilli. The sauce can be concentrated by cooking it for longer. Store in the refrigerator and add water or stock to thin it when reheating.*

Chop the vegetables into small, even-sized pieces before adding to the hot oil.

Dice the tomatoes into small pieces, before adding with the parsley, sugar and water.

NUTRITION PER SERVE (6)
Protein 10 g; Fat 7 g; Carbohydrate 65 g; Dietary Fibre 6 g; Cholesterol 0 mg; 1540 kJ (365 Cal)

Pasta carbonara

PREPARATION TIME: 15 MINUTES | TOTAL COOKING TIME: 25 MINUTES | SERVES 4–6

8 bacon slices

500 g (1 lb 2 oz) pasta (see NOTE)

4 eggs

310 ml (10¾ fl oz/1¼ cups) pouring (whipping) cream

60 g (2¼ oz) grated parmesan cheese, plus extra, to serve

1 Cut the bacon into thin strips. Cook over medium heat until crisp. Drain on paper towels. Meanwhile, cook the pasta in a large saucepan of rapidly boiling salted water until *al dente*. Drain well and return to the pan to keep warm.

2 Beat the eggs, cream and parmesan together and season well. Stir in the bacon. Pour over the hot pasta in the saucepan and toss gently until the sauce coats the pasta. Return to very low heat and cook for about 1 minute, or until the sauce has thickened slightly. Don't increase the heat or the eggs will scramble. Season with freshly ground black pepper and serve immediately with extra grated parmesan cheese.

NOTE: *Traditionally, spaghetti or fettuccine is served with this sauce. We have shown tagliatelle.*

Cook the bacon strips, stirring, until they are crisp, being careful not to let them burn.

After beating together the eggs, cream and parmesan, stir in the cooked bacon.

NUTRITION PER SERVE (6)
Protein 22 g; Fat 36 g; Carbohydrate 60 g; Dietary Fibre 4 g; Cholesterol 213.5 mg; 2700 kJ (645 Cal)

Pasta puttanesca

PREPARATION TIME: 15 MINUTES | TOTAL COOKING TIME: 20 MINUTES | SERVES 4–6

500 g (1 lb 2 oz) spaghetti or fettuccine
2 tablespoons olive oil
3 garlic cloves, crushed
2 tablespoons chopped parsley
¼–½ teaspoon chilli flakes, or chilli powder
850 g (1 lb 14 oz) tinned chopped tomatoes
1 tablespoon capers, rinsed and drained
3 anchovy fillets, chopped
3 tablespoons black olives

NUTRITION PER SERVE (6)
Protein 11 g; Fat 7 g; Carbohydrate 63 g; Dietary
Fibre 6 g; Cholesterol 0 mg; 1549 kJ (370 Cal)

1 Cook the spaghetti or fettuccine in a large saucepan of rapidly boiling salted water until *al dente.* Drain well and return to the pan to keep warm.

2 Meanwhile, heat the oil in a heavy-based frying pan. Add the garlic, parsley and chilli flakes and cook, stirring, for 1 minute over medium heat.

3 Add the tomato and stir to combine. Reduce the heat and simmer, covered, for 5 minutes.

4 Add the capers, anchovies and olives and cook, stirring, for 5 minutes. Season with freshly ground black pepper. Add the sauce to the pasta and toss together gently. Serve immediately.

HINT: *If you can't find tins of chopped tomatoes, use tinned whole tomatoes—simply chop in the tin with a pair of kitchen scissors.*

Cook the garlic, parsley and chilli flakes over medium heat for 1 minute.

Add the tomato to the garlic, parsley and chilli flakes.

Add the capers, anchovies and olives and stir for 5 minutes.

Pasta arrabbiata

PREPARATION TIME: 30 MINUTES | TOTAL COOKING TIME: 50 MINUTES | SERVES 4

75 g (2½ oz/½ cup) bacon fat
2–3 red chillies
2 tablespoons olive oil
1 large onion, finely chopped
1 garlic clove, finely chopped
500 g (1 lb 2 oz) very ripe tomatoes, finely
    chopped
500 g (1 lb 2 oz) pasta (see NOTE)
2 tablespoons chopped parsley
grated parmesan cheese or pecorino cheese,
    for serving

1 Use a large knife to finely chop the bacon fat. Chop the chillies, taking care to avoid skin irritation—wearing rubber gloves will help. Heat the oil in a heavy-based frying pan and add the bacon fat, chilli, onion and garlic. Fry for 8 minutes, stirring occasionally.

2 Add the tomato to the pan with 125 ml (4 fl oz/½ cup) water and season to taste. Cover and simmer for about 40 minutes, or until the sauce is thick and rich.

3 When the sauce is almost cooked, cook the pasta in a large saucepan of rapidly boiling salted water until *al dente*. Drain well and return to the pan to keep warm.

4 Add the parsley to the sauce and toss gently through the pasta. Serve with the parmesan cheese or pecorino cheese sprinkled over the top, if desired.

NOTE: *Penne rigate is traditionally served with this sauce. We have used papardelle.*

Remove the stalks and slice the chillies in half. Wear rubber gloves to protect your skin.

The chilli seeds and membrane are left in as this is a fiery sauce, but remove them if you prefer.

NUTRITION PER SERVE
Protein 20 g; Fat 25 g; Carbohydrate 95 g; Dietary Fibre 9 g; Cholesterol 20 mg; 2880 kJ (685 Cal)

Spinach and ricotta gnocchi

PREPARATION TIME: 45 MINUTES + 1 HOUR REFRIGERATION | TOTAL COOKING TIME: 15 MINUTES | SERVES 4–6

4 slices white bread
125 ml (4 fl oz/½ cup) milk
500 g (1 lb 2 oz) frozen spinach, thawed
250 g (9 oz/1 cup) ricotta cheese
2 eggs
60 g (2¼ oz) grated parmesan cheese
30 g (1 oz/¼ cup) plain (all-purpose) flour
shaved parmesan cheese, for serving

GARLIC BUTTER SAUCE
100 g (3½ oz) salted butter
2 garlic cloves, crushed
3 tablespoons chopped basil
1 ripe tomato, diced

1 Remove the crusts from the bread and soak in milk in a shallow dish for 10 minutes. Squeeze out any excess milk from the bread. Squeeze out any excess liquid from the spinach.

2 Place the bread, spinach, ricotta, eggs and parmesan in a bowl and mix thoroughly. Refrigerate, covered, for 1 hour. Fold the flour in well.

3 Lightly dust your hands in flour and roll heaped teaspoons of the bread mixture into dumplings. Lower batches of the gnocchi into a large saucepan of boiling salted water. Cook each batch for about 2 minutes, or until the gnocchi rise to the surface. Transfer to a serving plate and keep warm.

4 To make the sauce, combine all the ingredients in a small saucepan and cook over medium heat for 3 minutes, or until the butter is nutty brown. Drizzle over the gnocchi and sprinkle with the parmesan.

NUTRITION PER SERVE (6)
Protein 17 g; Fat 26 g; Carbohydrate 16 g; Dietary Fibre 5 g; Cholesterol 137 mg; 1504 kJ (360 Cal)

Gently squeeze out any excess milk from the soaked bread.

With floured hands, roll teaspoons of the mixture into dumplings.

Soups

Bean soup with sausage

PREPARATION TIME: 25 MINUTES I TOTAL COOKING TIME: 30 MINUTES I SERVES 4–6

2 teaspoons olive oil

4 Italian sausages, diced

2 leeks, sliced

1 garlic clove, crushed

1 large carrot, finely diced

2 celery stalks, sliced

2 tablespoons plain (all-purpose) flour

2 beef stock (bouillon) cubes, crumbled

125 ml (4 fl oz/½ cup) dry white wine

125 g (4½ oz) small pasta shells

440 g (15½ oz) tinned three-bean mix,
    drained and rinsed

1 teaspoon chopped chilli (optional)

1   Heat the oil in a large heavy-based saucepan and add the sausage. Cook over medium heat for 5 minutes or until golden, stirring regularly. Drain on paper towels.

2   Add the leek, garlic, carrot and celery to the pan and cook, stirring occasionally, for 2–3 minutes or until soft.

3   Add the flour and cook, stirring, for 1 minute. Add the stock cubes and wine and gradually stir in 2 litres (70 fl oz/8 cups) water. Bring to the boil, then reduce the heat and simmer for 10 minutes.

4   Add the pasta, beans and chilli (if using) to the pan. Increase the heat and cook for 8–10 minutes, or until the pasta is *al dente*. Return the sausage to the saucepan and season to taste.

NUTRITION PER SERVE (6)
Protein 10 g; Fat 4 g; Carbohydrate 30 g; Dietary Fibre 8 g; Cholesterol 7 mg; 888 kJ (212 Cal)

VARIATION: *Use dried beans, if preferred. Place in a bowl; cover with water; soak overnight. Drain; add to a large saucepan with water to come about 3 cm (1¼ inches) above the beans; simmer for 1 hour. Drain well before adding to the soup.*

Cook the sausage pieces over medium heat for 5 minutes, or until golden.

Add the leek, garlic, carrot and celery and cook, stirring occasionally, until soft.

Add the stock and then the wine and water and bring to the boil.

Chicken and vegetable soup

PREPARATION TIME: 15 MINUTES | TOTAL COOKING TIME: 20 MINUTES | SERVES 4

1 tablespoon oil
1 carrot, sliced
1 leek, chopped
2 boneless, skinless chicken thighs, cut into
   bite-sized pieces
35 g (1¼ oz/¼ cup) ditalini or other small
   pasta
1 litre (35 fl oz/4 cups) vegetable stock
2 ripe tomatoes, diced

1 Heat the oil in a saucepan and cook the carrot and leek over medium heat for 4 minutes, or until soft. Add the chicken and cook for a further 2 minutes, or until the chicken has changed colour.

2 Add the pasta and the vegetable stock, cover and bring to the boil. Reduce the heat and simmer for 10 minutes, or until the pasta is cooked. Add the tomato halfway through the cooking. Season to taste with salt and pepper. Serve with fresh crusty bread.

Cook the carrot and leek until they are soft, then add the chicken and cook until it changes colour.

Add the pasta to the soup and simmer for 10 minutes, or until it is tender.

NUTRITION PER SERVE
Protein 20 g; Fat 7 g; Carbohydrate 9 g; Dietary
Fibre 2 g; Cholesterol 40 mg; 725 kJ (173 Cal)

Country pumpkin and pasta soup

PREPARATION TIME: 25 MINUTES | TOTAL COOKING TIME: 20 MINUTES | SERVES 4–6

750 g (1 lb 10 oz) pumpkin (winter squash)
2 all-purpose potatoes
1 tablespoon olive oil
30 g (1 oz) salted butter
1 large onion, finely chopped
2 garlic cloves, crushed
3 litres (105 fl oz/12 cups) chicken stock
125 g (4½ oz) miniature pasta or risoni
1 tablespoon chopped parsley, for serving

1 Peel the pumpkin and potatoes and chop into small cubes. Heat the oil and butter in a large saucepan. Add the onion and garlic and cook, stirring, for 5 minutes over low heat.

2 Add the pumpkin, potato and chicken stock. Increase the heat, cover and cook for 8 minutes, or until the vegetables are tender.

3 Add the pasta and cook, stirring occasionally, for 5 minutes or until the pasta is *al dente*. Serve immediately, sprinkled with the chopped parsley.

NOTES: *Butternut or jap (kent) pumpkin will give this soup the sweetest flavour.*

Tiny star-shaped pasta look attractive in this soup.

NUTRITION PER SERVE (6)
Protein 6 g; Fat 5 g; Carbohydrate 30 g; Dietary Fibre 3 g; Cholesterol 13 mg; 782 kJ (187 Cal)

Peel the pumpkin and potatoes and chop them into small cubes.

Add the pumpkin, potato and chicken stock, then cover the pan.

Add the pasta and cook, stirring occasionally until it is *al dente*.

Spicy chicken broth with coriander pasta

PREPARATION TIME: 40 MINUTES | TOTAL COOKING TIME: 50 MINUTES | SERVES 4

350 g (12 oz) boneless, skinless chicken
   thighs or wings
2 carrots, finely chopped
2 celery stalks, finely chopped
2 small leeks, finely chopped
3 egg whites
1.5 litres (52 fl oz/6 cups) chicken stock
Tabasco sauce

CORIANDER PASTA
60 g (2¼ oz/½ cup) plain (all-purpose) flour
1 egg
½ teaspoon sesame oil
75 g (2½ oz) coriander (cilantro) leaves

1   Put the chicken and vegetables in a large heavy-based saucepan. Push the chicken to one side and add the egg whites to the vegetables. Using a wire whisk, beat until frothy.

2   Warm the stock in another saucepan, gradually add to the first pan, whisking continuously to froth the egg whites. Continue whisking while slowly bringing to the boil. Make a hole in the froth on top with a spoon and leave to simmer, uncovered, for 30 minutes without stirring.

3   Line a sieve with a damp tea towel (dish towel) or double thickness of muslin (cheesecloth) and strain the broth into a clean bowl (discard chicken and vegetables). Season with salt, pepper and Tabasco. Set aside.

4   To make the pasta, sift the flour into a bowl and make a well in the centre. Whisk the egg and oil together and pour into the well. Mix to make a dough and knead on a lightly floured surface for 2 minutes, until smooth. Divide into four portions. Roll one out very thinly and cover with a layer of evenly spaced coriander leaves. Roll out another and lay this on top of the leaves, then gently roll the layers together. Repeat with the remaining pasta and coriander.

5   Cut out squares of pasta around the leaves. Heat the broth gently in a saucepan. Add the pasta and cook for 1 minute. Serve immediately.

NOTE: *The egg whites make the broth clear. This is called clarifying the stock. Making a hole in the froth prevents the stock boiling over.*

NUTRITION PER SERVE
Protein 25 g; Fat 4 g; Carbohydrate 18 g; Dietary
Fibre 4 g; Cholesterol 90 mg; 915 kJ (220 Cal)

Use a wire whisk to beat the egg white and vegetables until frothy.

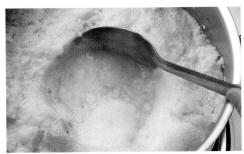
Use a metal spoon to make a hole in the froth on top of the soup.

Strain the broth through a damp tea towel or double thickness of muslin.

Tomato ditalini soup

PREPARATION TIME: 15 MINUTES | TOTAL COOKING TIME: 20 MINUTES | SERVES 4

2 tablespoons olive oil
1 large onion, finely chopped
2 celery stalks, finely chopped
3 vine-ripened tomatoes
1.5 litres (52 fl oz/6 cups) chicken or
  vegetable stock
90 g (3¼ oz/½ cup) ditalini
2 tablespoons chopped parsley

1 Heat the oil in a large saucepan over medium heat. Add the onion and celery and cook for 5 minutes, or until they have softened.

2 Score a cross in the base of each tomato, then place in a bowl of boiling water for 1 minute. Plunge the tomatoes into cold water and peel the skin away from the cross. Halve the tomatoes and scoop out the seeds with a teaspoon. Roughly chop the flesh.

3 Add the stock and tomato to the pan and bring to the boil. Add the pasta and cook for 10 minutes, or until *al dente*. Season and sprinkle with parsley. Serve with crusty bread.

NUTRITION PER SERVE
Protein 8 g; Fat 11 g; Carbohydrate 23 g; Dietary Fibre 3.5 g; Cholesterol 0 mg; 925 kJ (220 Cal)

Peel the tomatoes by plunging in boiling water, then scoop out the seeds.

Simple vegetable and pasta soup

PREPARATION TIME: 20 MINUTES I TOTAL COOKING TIME: 40 MINUTES I SERVES 6

2 teaspoons olive oil
1 onion, chopped
1 carrot, chopped
2 celery stalks, chopped
350 g (12 oz) sweet potato, chopped
400 g (14 oz) tinned corn kernels, drained
1 litre (35 fl oz/4 cups) vegetable stock
90 g (3¼ oz/1 cup) pasta spirals

1 Heat the oil in a large saucepan and add the onion, carrot and celery. Cook over low heat, stirring regularly, for 10 minutes, or until soft.

2 Add the sweet potato, corn kernels and stock. Bring to the boil, reduce the heat and simmer for 20 minutes, or until the vegetables are tender.

3 Add the pasta to the pan and return to the boil. Reduce the heat and simmer for 10 minutes, or until the pasta is *al dente*. Serve immediately.

NUTRITION PER SERVE
Protein 4 g; Fat 2 g; Carbohydrate 25 g; Dietary Fibre 5 g; Cholesterol 0 mg; 555 kJ (135 Cal)

Stir the onion, carrot and celery over low heat, stirring regularly, until soft.

Add the sweet potato, corn kernels and the stock.

When the vegetables are tender, add the pasta to the saucepan.

Minestrone with pesto

PREPARATION TIME: 25 MINUTES + OVERNIGHT SOAKING | TOTAL COOKING TIME: 2 HOURS | SERVES 6

125 g (4½ oz) dried borlotti beans
1 large onion, roughly chopped
2 garlic cloves
3 tablespoons chopped parsley
60 g (2¼ oz) pancetta, chopped
3 tablespoons olive oil
1 celery stalk, halved lengthways, then cut into 1 cm (½ inch) slices
1 carrot, halved lengthways, then cut into 1 cm (½ inch) slices
1 all-purpose potato, diced
2 teaspoons tomato paste (concentrated purée)
400 g (14 oz) tinned chopped tomatoes
6 basil leaves, roughly torn
2 litres (70 fl oz/8 cups) chicken or vegetable stock
2 thin zucchini (courgettes), cut into thick slices
120 g (4¼ oz/¾ cup) shelled fresh peas
60 g (2¼ oz/½ cup) green beans, cut into short lengths
90 g (3¼ oz) silverbeet (Swiss chard) leaves, shredded
75 g (2½ oz) ditalini or other small pasta

PESTO
1 very large handful basil leaves
1 tablespoon lightly toasted pine nuts
2 garlic cloves
100 ml (3½ fl oz) olive oil
30 g (1 oz) grated parmesan cheese

1 Put the borlotti beans in a large bowl, cover with water and soak overnight. Drain and rinse under cold water.

2 Put the onion, garlic, parsley and pancetta in a food processor and process until fine. Heat the oil in a saucepan, add the pancetta mixture and cook over low heat, stirring occasionally, for 8–10 minutes.

3 Add the celery, carrot and potato, and cook for 5 minutes, then stir in the tomato paste, tomato, basil and borlotti beans. Season with freshly ground black pepper. Add the stock and bring slowly to the boil. Cover and simmer, stirring occasionally, for 1 hour 30 minutes.

4 Season and add the zucchini, peas, green beans, silverbeet and pasta. Simmer for 8–10 minutes, or until the vegetables and pasta are *al dente*.

5 To make the pesto, combine the basil, pine nuts and garlic with a pinch of salt in a food processor. Process until finely chopped. With the motor running, slowly add the olive oil. Transfer to a bowl and stir in the parmesan and freshly ground black pepper to taste. Serve the soup in bowls with the pesto on top.

NUTRITION PER SERVE
Protein 9 g; Fat 30 g; Carbohydrate 20 g; Dietary Fibre 5.3 g; Cholesterol 9 mg; 1593 kJ (380 Cal)

Cook the processed onion, garlic, parsley and pancetta mixture.

Simmer until the pasta and vegetables are *al dente*.

Stir the parmesan and black pepper into the pesto and serve with the soup.

Pasta and white bean soup

PREPARATION TIME: 30 MINUTES | TOTAL COOKING TIME: 20 MINUTES | SERVES 6

PESTO
50 g (1¾ oz/⅓ cup) pine nuts
2 large handfuls basil leaves
50 g (1¾ oz) rocket (arugula) leaves
2 garlic cloves, chopped
35 g (1¼ oz/⅓ cup) finely grated parmesan
    cheese
4 tablespoons olive oil

185 g (6½ oz) spiral pasta
1.5 litres (52 fl oz/6 cups) chicken stock
600 g (1 lb 5 oz) tinned cannellini beans,
    drained and rinsed (see NOTE)

1   Put the pine nuts in a dry frying pan and
toast them over medium heat for 1–2 minutes, or
until golden brown. Remove from the pan and
allow to cool.

2   To make the pesto, mix the pine nuts, basil,
rocket, garlic and parmesan in a food processor
and process until finely chopped. With the motor
running, add the oil in a thin stream until well
combined. Season to taste with salt and pepper.
Set aside.

3   Cook the pasta in rapidly boiling salted water
until *al dente*. Heat the chicken stock in a large
saucepan until it begins to boil. Reduce the heat
to simmering point. Drain the pasta and add to
the stock with the cannellini beans. Reheat and
serve with a spoonful of pesto.

NOTE: *Cannellini beans are small, white and
slightly kidney-shaped and are much used in
Italian cooking, particularly in Tuscany.*

Dry-fry the pine nuts until golden brown, but take
care not to let them burn.

Put the pine nuts, basil, rocket, garlic and
parmesan cheese in a food processor.

NUTRITION PER SERVE
Protein 15 g; Fat 20 g; Carbohydrate 40 g; Dietary
Fibre 4 g; Cholesterol 5 mg; 1770 kJ (425 Cal)

Ratatouille and pasta soup

PREPARATION TIME: 25 MINUTES | TOTAL COOKING TIME: 40 MINUTES | SERVES 6

1 eggplant (aubergine), chopped
1 tablespoon olive oil
1 large onion, chopped
1 large red capsicum (pepper), chopped
1 large green capsicum (pepper), chopped
2 garlic cloves, crushed
3 zucchini (courgettes), sliced
800 g (1 lb 12 oz) tinned chopped tomatoes
1 teaspoon dried oregano leaves
½ teaspoon dried thyme leaves
1 litre (35 fl oz/4 cups) vegetable stock
45 g (1½ oz) pasta spirals
parmesan cheese, to serve

1 Spread the eggplant out in a colander and sprinkle generously with salt. Leave for 20 minutes; rinse and pat dry with paper towels.

2 Heat the oil in a large heavy-based saucepan and cook the onion for 10 minutes, or until soft and lightly golden. Add the capsicum, garlic, zucchini and eggplant and cook for 5 minutes.

3 Add the tomato, herbs and stock to the pan. Bring to the boil, then reduce the heat and simmer for 10 minutes, or until the vegetables are tender. Add the pasta and cook for 15 minutes, until *al dente*. Serve with parmesan cheese and bread.

STORAGE: *This soup will keep for up to 2 days in the refrigerator.*

Put the chopped eggplant in a colander and sprinkle generously with salt.

Add the capsicum, garlic, zucchini and eggplant to the pan.

NUTRITION PER SERVE
Protein 6 g; Fat 4 g; Carbohydrate 23 g; Dietary Fibre 5 g; Cholesterol 0 mg; 635 kJ (150 Cal)

Lemon-scented broth with tortellini

PREPARATION TIME: 10 MINUTES | TOTAL COOKING TIME: 20 MINUTES | SERVES 4–6

1 lemon

125 ml (4 fl oz/½ cup) dry white wine

500 ml (17 fl oz/2 cups) tinned chicken consommé

1 very large handful chopped parsley

375 g (13 oz) fresh veal- or chicken-filled tortellini

1   Using a vegetable peeler, peel wide strips from the lemon. Remove the white pith with a small sharp knife and cut three of the wide lemon pieces into fine strips. Set these aside for garnishing.

2   Place the wide lemon strips, white wine, consommé and 750 ml (26 fl oz/3 cups) water in a large deep saucepan. Cook for 10 minutes over low heat. Remove the lemon zest and bring to the boil.

3   Add half the parsley, the tortellini and a sprinkling of black pepper to the pan. Cook for 6–7 minutes or until the pasta is *al dente*. Garnish with the remaining parsley and the fine strips of lemon.

STORAGE: *If you want, you can prepare this recipe up to the end of step 2 and then leave in the fridge for a day before adding the pasta.*

NUTRITION PER SERVE (6)
Protein 6 g; Fat 4 g; Carbohydrate 9 g; Dietary Fibre 2 g; Cholesterol 14 mg; 483 kJ (115 Cal)

Remove the wide strips of peel from the lemon and then remove the bitter white pith.

Cook for 10 minutes and then lift out the strips of lemon with a slotted spoon.

Bring the liquid to the boil and then add the parsley and tortellini.

Bacon and pea soup

PREPARATION TIME: 20 MINUTES I TOTAL COOKING TIME: 15 MINUTES I SERVES 4–6

4 slices bacon, diced
50 g (1¾ oz) salted butter
1 large onion, finely chopped
1 celery stalk, chopped into small pieces
2 litres (70 fl oz/8 cups) chicken stock
150 g (5½ oz/1 cup) frozen peas
250 g (9 oz) risoni
2 tablespoons chopped parsley

1   Put the bacon, butter, onion and celery in a large heavy-based saucepan. Cook for 5 minutes over low heat, stirring occasionally.

2   Add the stock and peas and simmer, covered, for 5 minutes. Increase the heat and add the pasta. Cook uncovered, stirring occasionally, for 5 minutes. Add the parsley and serve.

STORAGE: *Store in an airtight container in the refrigerator for up to a day. Gently reheat before serving.*

HINT: *Double-smoked bacon will give the best flavour for this recipe.*

NUTRITION PER SERVE (6)
Protein 10 g; Fat 9 g; Carbohydrate 35 g; Dietary Fibre 4 g; Cholesterol 28 mg; 1066 kJ (255 Cal)

Remove any excess fat from the bacon before you dice it.

Cook the bacon, butter, onion and celery in a large saucepan for 5 minutes.

Just before you serve the soup, add the chopped parsley to the pan.

Hearty Italian bean and pasta soup

PREPARATION TIME: **15** MINUTES | TOTAL COOKING TIME: **20** MINUTES | SERVES **4**

1 tablespoon olive oil

1 onion, finely chopped

3 garlic cloves, crushed

600 g (1 lb 5 oz) tinned mixed beans, drained
   and rinsed

1.75 litres (61 fl oz/7 cups) chicken stock
   (see NOTE)

100 g (3½ oz) conchigliette (small pasta shells)

1 tablespoon chopped tarragon

1   Heat the oil in a saucepan over low heat. Add
the onion and cook for 5 minutes, then add the
garlic and cook for a further 1 minute, stirring
frequently. Add the beans and chicken stock and
then cover the pan with a lid.

2   Increase the heat and bring to the boil.
Add the pasta and cook until *al dente*. Stir in
the tarragon, then season with salt and freshly
ground black pepper. Serve with crusty bread.

NOTE: *The flavour of this soup is really enhanced
by using a good-quality stock. Either make your
own or use the cartons of liquid stock that are
available at the supermarket.*

NUTRITION PER SERVE
Protein 12 g; Fat 6.5 g; Carbohydrate 34 g; Dietary
Fibre 8 g; Cholesterol 0 mg; 1015 kJ (240 Cal)

Add the beans and chicken stock, cover the pan
and bring to the boil.

Lamb and pasta soup

PREPARATION TIME: 10 MINUTES I TOTAL COOKING TIME: 40 MINUTES I SERVES 6–8

2 tablespoons oil
500 g (1 lb 2 oz) lean lamb, cut into
    bite-sized cubes
2 onions, finely chopped
2 carrots, chopped
4 celery stalks, chopped
425 g (15 oz) tinned chopped tomatoes
2 litres (70 fl oz/8 cups) beef stock
300 g (10½ oz) spiral pasta
chopped parsley, for serving

1 Heat the oil in a large saucepan and cook the lamb in batches until golden brown. Remove each batch as it is cooked and drain on paper towels. Add the onion to the pan and cook for 2 minutes or until softened. Return all the meat to the pan.

2 Add the carrot, celery, tomato and beef stock. Stir to combine and bring to the boil. Reduce the heat to low and simmer, covered, for 15 minutes.

3 Add the spiral pasta to the soup. Stir briefly to prevent the pasta sticking to the pan. Simmer, uncovered, for another 15 minutes or until the lamb and pasta are tender. Sprinkle with chopped parsley before serving.

STORAGE: *This soup can be kept, covered, in the refrigerator for up to 3 days.*

HINT: *If you prefer, the pasta can be cooked separately, drained and added to the soup just before serving.*

VARIATIONS: *For a lighter flavour, use half stock and half water. Vegetable stock can be used instead of beef.*

NUTRITION PER SERVE (8)
Protein 20 g; Fat 8 g; Carbohydrate 34 g; Dietary Fibre 4 g; Cholesterol 41 mg; 1195 kJ (285 Cal)

Cook the lamb in batches so that it browns without stewing.

Add the carrot, celery, tomato and beef stock to the saucepan.

Add the spiral pasta to the soup and stir briefly to prevent it sticking.

Pasta with meat

Mediterranean pasta

PREPARATION TIME: 15 MINUTES I TOTAL COOKING TIME: 1 HOUR 5 MINUTES I SERVES 4

2 tablespoons olive oil

1 teaspoon dried oregano

2 garlic cloves, finely chopped

6 roma (plum) tomatoes, halved

500 g (1 lb 2 oz) spaghetti

4 slices prosciutto

16 kalamata olives

200 g (7 oz) feta cheese, cut into bite-sized cubes

1 tablespoon balsamic vinegar

100 ml (3½ fl oz) olive oil, extra

3 garlic cloves, thinly sliced, extra

60 g (2¼ oz) rocket (arugula) leaves

NUTRITION PER SERVE
Protein 14 g; Fat 40 g; Carbohydrate 75 g; Dietary Fibre 9 g; Cholesterol 2.5 mg; 3020 kJ (720 Cal)

1 Preheat the oven to 150°C (300°F/Gas 2). Combine the olive oil, oregano, garlic and 1 teaspoon salt in a bowl. Add the tomato and toss to combine, rubbing the mixture onto the cut halves of the tomatoes. Place the tomato cut side up on a lined baking tray and cook in the oven for 1 hour.

2 Meanwhile, cook the pasta in a large saucepan of rapidly boiling salted water until *al dente*. Drain well and return to the pan to keep warm. Place the prosciutto on a grill tray and cook under a hot grill (broiler), turning once, for 3–4 minutes, or until crispy. Break into pieces.

3 Toss the tomato, olives, feta, spaghetti and balsamic vinegar in a bowl and keep warm.

4 Heat the extra olive oil in a small saucepan and cook the extra garlic over low heat, without burning, for 1–2 minutes, or until the garlic has infused the oil.

5 Pour the garlic and oil over the spaghetti mixture, add the rocket leaves and toss well. Sprinkle with the prosciutto pieces and season well. Serve immediately.

Rub the olive oil, oregano, garlic and salt mixture into the cut halves of the tomato.

Grill the prosciutto until crispy, then break into small pieces.

Toss the tomato, olives, feta, spaghetti and balsamic vinegar in a bowl.

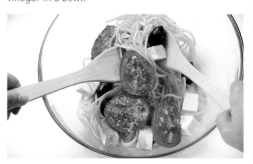

Italian omelette

PREPARATION TIME: 20 MINUTES | TOTAL COOKING TIME: 15 MINUTES | SERVES 4

2 tablespoons olive oil
1 onion, finely chopped
155 g (5½ oz/1 cup) sliced ham, chopped
6 eggs
3 tablespoons milk
350 g (12 oz/2 cups) cooked fusilli or spiral
    pasta (see NOTE)
25 g (1 oz/¼ cup) grated parmesan cheese
2 tablespoons chopped parsley
1 tablespoon chopped basil
60 g (2¼ oz/½ cup) grated cheddar cheese

1 Heat half the oil in a frying pan. Add the onion and stir over low heat until tender. Add the ham and stir for 1 minute. Transfer to a plate.

2 Whisk together the eggs and milk and season. Stir in the pasta, parmesan, herbs and onion mixture.

3 Preheat the grill (broiler) to hot. Heat the remaining oil in the same pan. Pour the egg mixture into the pan. Sprinkle with the cheddar cheese. Cook over medium heat until the omelette begins to set around the edges then place under the grill until lightly browned on top. Cut into wedges for serving.

NOTE: *To get 2 cups of cooked pasta you will need to start with about 150 g (5½ oz) of uncooked dried pasta.*

Whisk together the eggs and milk, then stir in the pasta, parmesan, herbs and onion mixture.

Pour into the pan and then sprinkle with the cheddar. Finish cooking under the grill.

NUTRITION PER SERVE
Protein 30 g; Fat 32 g; Carbohydrate 30 g; Dietary Fibre 2 g; Cholesterol 327 mg; 2206 kJ (530 Cal)

Bucatini with sausage and fennel seed

PREPARATION TIME: 10 MINUTES | TOTAL COOKING TIME: 40 MINUTES | SERVES 4

500 g (1 lb 2 oz) Italian sausages
2 tablespoons olive oil
3 garlic cloves, chopped
1 teaspoon fennel seeds
½ teaspoon chilli flakes
850 g (1 lb 14 oz) tinned chopped tomatoes
500 g (1 lb 2 oz) bucatini
1 teaspoon balsamic vinegar
1 small handful basil, chopped

1   Heat a frying pan over high heat, add the sausages and cook, turning regularly, for 8–10 minutes, or until well browned and cooked through. Remove, cool slightly and slice thinly on the diagonal.

2   Heat the oil in a saucepan, add the garlic and cook over medium heat for 1 minute. Add the fennel seeds and chilli flakes and cook for a further minute. Stir in the tomato and bring to the boil, then reduce the heat and simmer, covered, for 20 minutes. Meanwhile, cook the pasta in a large saucepan of rapidly boiling salted water until *al dente*. Drain well and return to the pan to keep warm.

3   Add the sausages to the sauce and cook, uncovered, for 5 minutes to heat through. Stir in the balsamic vinegar and basil. Divide the pasta among four bowls, top with the sauce and serve.

NUTRITION PER SERVE
Protein 34 g; Fat 51 g; Carbohydrate 96 g; Dietary Fibre 10 g; Cholesterol 95 mg; 4125 kJ (985 Cal)

Fry the sausages until they are well browned then slice them on the diagonal.

Cook the garlic, fennel seeds and chilli flakes in the oil.

Fusilli with bacon and broad bean sauce

PREPARATION TIME: 30 MINUTES | TOTAL COOKING TIME: 25 MINUTES | SERVES 4–6

500 g (1 lb 2 oz) fusilli or penne
310 g (11 oz/2 cups) frozen broad (fava)
  beans
2 tablespoons olive oil
2 leeks, finely sliced
4 bacon slices, diced
310 ml (10¾ fl oz/1¼ cups) pouring
  (whipping) cream
2 teaspoons grated lemon zest

1 Cook the pasta in a large saucepan of rapidly boiling salted water until *al dente*. Drain well and return to the pan to keep warm. While the pasta is cooking, plunge the broad beans into a saucepan of boiling water. Remove with a slotted spoon and place immediately in cold water. Drain and allow to cool, then peel (see NOTE).

2 Heat the oil in a heavy-based frying pan. Add the leek and bacon and cook over medium heat, stirring occasionally, for 8 minutes, or until the leek is golden. Add the cream and lemon zest and cook for 2 minutes. Add the broad beans and season well.

3 Add the sauce to the pasta and toss to combine. Serve at once.

NOTE: *Broad beans can be cooked and peeled in advance and refrigerated in an airtight container until needed. To peel them, break off the top and squeeze out the beans. Leaving the hard outside skin on the broad bean will change the delicate texture and flavour of this dish—it is worth the extra effort to peel them. Very young fresh broad beans can be used without peeling.*

NUTRITION PER SERVE (6)
Protein 20 g; Fat 30 g; Carbohydrate 62 g; Dietary
Fibre 8 g; Cholesterol 83 mg; 2531 kJ (600 Cal)

Carefully remove the outer leaves and dark green section from the leeks. Clean them thoroughly.

After cooling the broad beans, peel away the outer skins.

Add the cream and the grated lemon zest to the leek and bacon in the pan.

Risoni risotto with mushrooms and pancetta

PREPARATION TIME: 15 MINUTES | TOTAL COOKING TIME: 35 MINUTES | SERVES 4–6

1 tablespoon salted butter

2 garlic cloves, finely chopped

150 g (5½ oz) piece pancetta, diced

400 g (14 oz) button mushrooms, sliced

500 g (1 lb 2 oz) risoni

1 litre (35 fl oz/ 4 cups) chicken stock

125 ml (4 fl oz/½ cup) pouring (whipping) cream

50 g (1¾ oz/½ cup) finely grated parmesan cheese

4 tablespoons finely chopped flat-leaf (Italian) parsley

1   Heat the butter in a saucepan, add the garlic and cook over medium heat for 30 seconds. Increase the heat to high, add the pancetta and cook for a further 3–5 minutes, or until crisp. Add the mushrooms and cook for 3–5 minutes, or until softened.

2   Add the risoni, stir until it is coated in the mixture, then add the stock and bring to the boil. Reduce the heat to medium and cook, covered, for 15–20 minutes, or until nearly all the liquid has evaporated and the risoni is tender.

3   Stir in the cream and cook, uncovered, for a further 3 minutes, stirring occasionally until the cream is absorbed. Stir in nearly all of the parmesan and all the parsley and season to taste. Divide among four serving bowls and serve with the remaining parmesan, if desired.

Cook the garlic and pancetta in the butter until the pancetta is crisp.

Add the risoni and stir until it is coated in the mixture, then add the stock.

NUTRITION PER SERVE (6)
Protein 21.5 g; Fat 20 g; Carbohydrate 60 g; Dietary Fibre 4.5 g; Cholesterol 60 mg; 2110 kJ (505 Cal)

Penne with rosemary and prosciutto

PREPARATION TIME: 15 MINUTES I TOTAL COOKING TIME: 25 MINUTES I SERVES 4–6

1 tablespoon olive oil
6 thin slices prosciutto, chopped
1 onion, finely chopped
820 g (1 lb 13 oz) tinned chopped tomatoes
1 tablespoon chopped rosemary
500 g (1 lb 2 oz) penne or macaroni
50 g (1¾ oz/½ cup) grated parmesan cheese,
    for serving

1   Heat the oil in a heavy-based frying pan. Add the prosciutto and onion and cook, stirring occasionally, over low heat for 5 minutes or until the prosciutto is golden and the onion has softened.

2   Add the tomatoes and rosemary to the pan, season with salt and pepper, and simmer for 10 minutes.

3   Meanwhile, cook the pasta in a large saucepan of rapidly boiling salted water until *al dente*. Drain well and return to the pan to keep warm. Divide among warmed serving bowls and top with the sauce. Sprinkle with parmesan and serve immediately.

NOTE: *Rosemary, commonly used in Mediterranean cookery, adds a distinctive flavour to this dish.*

NUTRITION PER SERVE (6)
Protein 40 g; Fat 8 g; Carbohydrate 65 g; Dietary Fibre 6 g; Cholesterol 13 mg; 1663 kJ (397 Cal)

If you can't find chopped tomatoes, use tinned whole tomatoes and chop them with scissors in the tin.

Cook the prosciutto and onion until the prosciutto is golden and the onion has softened.

Add the tomato and fresh rosemary to the sauce and season well.

Pappardelle with rabbit and capsicum

PREPARATION TIME: 20 MINUTES | TOTAL COOKING TIME: 2 HOURS | SERVES 4

3 tablespoons olive oil

1 x 1 kg (2 lb 4 oz) rabbit, jointed

2 bacon slices, chopped

1 onion, sliced

2 celery stalks, chopped

1 garlic clove, crushed

2 tablespoons plain (all-purpose) flour

1 teaspoon dried marjoram

425 g (15 oz) tinned chopped tomatoes

125 ml (4 fl oz/½ cup) dry red wine

3 tablespoons tomato paste (concentrated purée)

1 red capsicum (pepper), seeded and sliced

1 eggplant (aubergine), quartered and sliced

500 g (1 lb 2 oz) pappardelle

2 tablespoons grated parmesan cheese, for serving

1 Heat the oil in a large frying pan. Add the rabbit and brown well on all sides. Transfer to a plate. Add the bacon, onion, celery and garlic to the same pan and stir over low heat until the onion is soft.

2 Stir in the flour and marjoram and cook for 1 minute. Add the tomato, wine, tomato paste, 125 ml (4 fl oz/½ cup) water and seaason with salt and pepper. Stir well.

3 Bring to the boil, stirring constantly. Reduce the heat and return the rabbit to the pan. Simmer, covered, for 1½ hours or until the rabbit is very tender, adding more water as required. Remove the rabbit from the sauce and allow to cool slightly. Remove the meat from the bones.

4 Return the rabbit meat to the sauce with the capsicum and eggplant. Simmer for another 15–20 minutes. Meanwhile, cook the pasta in a large saucepan of rapidly boiling salted water until *al dente*. Drain well and return to the pan to keep warm. Serve the hot sauce over the pasta, sprinkled with a little parmesan cheese, if desired.

NUTRITION PER SERVE
Protein 80 g; Fat 13 g; Carbohydrate 102 g; Dietary Fibre 11 g; Cholesterol 166 mg; 3690 kJ (880 Cal)

Heat the oil in a large frying pan and brown the rabbit on all sides.

Stir in the flour and dried marjoram and cook for a minute.

Add the tomato, wine, tomato paste, salt, pepper and water to the pan.

Low-fat linguine with bacon, mushrooms and peas

PREPARATION TIME: 20 MINUTES I TOTAL COOKING TIME: 25 MINUTES I SERVES 4

3 bacon slices
2 teaspoons olive oil
2–3 garlic cloves, crushed
1 red onion, chopped
185 g (6½ oz) field mushrooms, sliced
1 very large handful chopped parsley
150 g (5½ oz/1 cup) peas
375 ml (13 fl oz/1½ cups) low-fat light
    evaporated milk
2 teaspoons cornflour (cornstarch)
325 g (11½ oz) linguine
25 g (1 oz) shaved parmesan cheese

1 Remove the fat from the bacon and chop roughly. Heat the oil in a saucepan, add the garlic, onion and bacon and cook over low heat for 5 minutes, stirring frequently, until the onion and bacon are soft. Add the sliced mushrooms and cook, stirring, for another 5 minutes, or until soft.

2 Add the parsley, peas and milk to the pan. Mix the cornflour with 1 tablespoon water until smooth, add to the mixture and stir over medium heat until slightly thickened.

3 Cook the pasta in a large saucepan of rapidly boiling salted water until *al dente.* Drain well and serve with the hot sauce and parmesan cheese shavings.

NOTE: *Parmesan cheese adds a nice flavour to this dish, but leave it out if you are wanting a meal with a very low-fat content.*

Discard the fat from the bacon and chop the meat roughly into strips.

When the onion and bacon are softened, add the sliced mushrooms and stir while cooking.

NUTRITION PER SERVE
Protein 30 g; Fat 7 g; Carbohydrate 80 g; Dietary Fibre 9 g; Cholesterol 25 mg; 2085 kJ (500 Cal)

Penne with pumpkin, baked ricotta and prosciutto

PREPARATION TIME: 15 MINUTES | TOTAL COOKING TIME: 15 MINUTES | SERVES 4

500 g (1 lb 2 oz) penne

450 g (1 lb) butternut pumpkin (squash), cut into small cubes

3 tablespoons extra virgin olive oil

2 garlic cloves, crushed

100 g (3½ oz) semi-dried (sun-blushed) tomatoes, chopped

4 prosciutto slices, chopped

250 g (9 oz/1 cup) baked ricotta cheese, cut into small cubes

3 tablespoons shredded basil leaves

1   Cook the pasta in a large saucepan of rapidly boiling salted water until *al dente*. Drain well. Meanwhile, cook the pumpkin in a saucepan of boiling water for 10–12 minutes, or until just tender, then drain.

2   Heat the oil in a large saucepan, add the garlic and cook over medium heat for 30 seconds. Add the tomato, prosciutto, pumpkin and penne and toss gently over low heat for 1–2 minutes, or until heated through.

3   Add the baked ricotta and the basil, season with salt and freshly ground black pepper and serve immediately.

NUTRITION PER SERVE
Protein 28.5 g; Fat 23 g; Carbohydrate 99 g; Dietary Fibre 8.5 g; Cholesterol 37 mg; 3020 kJ (720 Cal)

Cook the pumpkin in boiling water until it is just tender, then drain.

Add the tomato, prosciutto, pumpkin and penne to the garlic and toss gently.

Add the baked ricotta and shredded fresh basil to the pasta and toss together.

Penne with veal ragù

PREPARATION TIME: 15 MINUTES | TOTAL COOKING TIME: 2 HOURS 40 MINUTES | SERVES 4

2 onions, sliced
2 bay leaves, crushed
1.5 kg (3 lb 5 oz) veal shin, cut into osso
    bucco pieces (see NOTE)
250 ml (9 fl oz/1 cup) dry red wine
800 g (1 lb 12 oz) tinned chopped tomatoes
375 m (13 fl oz/1½ cups) beef stock
2 teaspoons chopped rosemary
400 g (14 oz) penne
155 g (5½ oz/1 cup) frozen peas

1 Preheat the oven to 220°C (425°F/Gas 7). Scatter the onion over the bottom of a large roasting tin, lightly spray with oil and place the bay leaves and veal pieces on top. Season with salt and pepper. Roast for 10–15 minutes, or until the veal is browned. Take care that the onion doesn't burn.

2 Pour the wine over the veal and return to the oven for a further 5 minutes. Reduce the heat to 180°C (350°F/Gas 4), remove the tin from the oven and pour on the tomato, stock and 1 teaspoon of the rosemary. Cover with foil and return to the oven. Cook for 2 hours, or until the veal is starting to fall from the bone. Remove the foil and cook for a further 15 minutes, or until the meat loosens more from the bone and the liquid has evaporated slightly.

3 Cook the pasta in a large saucepan of rapidly boiling salted water until *al dente*. Drain well and return to the pan to keep warm. Meanwhile, remove the veal from the oven and cool slightly. Add the peas and remaining rosemary and place over a hotplate. Cook over medium heat for 5 minutes, or until the peas are cooked. Serve the pasta topped with the ragù.

NOTE: *Most butchers sell veal shin cut into osso bucco pieces. If sold in a whole piece, ask the butcher to cut it for you (the pieces are about 3–4 cm (1¼–1½ inches) thick). It is also available at some supermarkets. You can either remove the meat from the bone before serving, or leave it on.*

NUTRITION PER SERVE
Protein 52 g; Fat 5 g; Carbohydrate 81 g; Dietary Fibre 10 g; Cholesterol 125 mg; 2605 kJ (620 Cal)

Place the bay leaves and veal on top of the onion in the tin and roast until the veal is brown.

Cook the veal, covered and then uncovered, until it is falling away from the bone.

Add the frozen peas to the ragù and cook over medium heat for 5 minutes.

Penne with bacon, sun-dried tomatoes and lemon

PREPARATION TIME: 10 MINUTES | TOTAL COOKING TIME: 20 MINUTES | SERVES 4

250 g (9 oz) penne
3 tablespoons olive oil
3 bacon slices, chopped
1 onion, chopped
4 tablespoons lemon juice
1 tablespoon thyme leaves
50 g (1¾ oz/⅓ cup) chopped sun-dried
   tomatoes
80 g (2¾ oz/½ cup) pine nuts, toasted

1 Cook the pasta in a large saucepan of rapidly boiling salted water until *al dente*. Drain well and return to the pan to keep warm.

2 Heat the oil in a large saucepan. Add the bacon and onion and stir over medium heat for 4 minutes or until the bacon is brown and the onion has softened. Add the pasta, lemon juice, thyme, tomato and pine nuts. Stir over low heat for 2 minutes to heat through. Serve immediately.

HINT: *Sun-dried tomatoes will become bitter if heated too much.*

VARIATION: *Use pancetta instead of bacon, if preferred.*

NUTRITION PER SERVE
Protein 13 g; Fat 25 g; Carbohydrate 47 g; Dietary Fibre 5 g; Cholesterol 10 mg; 1972 kJ (471 Cal)

Add the pasta to the pan with the lemon juice, thyme, tomato and pine nuts.

Pasta with creamy tomato and bacon sauce

PREPARATION TIME: 10 MINUTES | TOTAL COOKING TIME: 15 MINUTES | SERVES 4

400 g (14 oz) pasta

1 tablespoon olive oil

180 g (6¼ oz) streaky bacon, thinly sliced (see NOTE)

500 g (1 lb 2 oz) roma (plum) tomatoes, roughly chopped

125 ml (4 fl oz/½ cup) thickened (whipping) cream

2 tablespoons sun-dried tomato pesto

2 tablespoons finely chopped flat-leaf (Italian) parsley

50 g (1¾ oz/½ cup) finely grated parmesan cheese

1 Cook the pasta in a large saucepan of rapidly boiling salted water until *al dente*. Drain well and return to the pan to keep warm. Meanwhile, heat the oil in a frying pan, add the bacon and cook over high heat for 2 minutes, or until starting to brown. Reduce the heat to medium, add the tomato and cook, stirring frequently, for 2 minutes, or until the tomato has softened but still holds its shape.

2 Add the cream and tomato pesto and stir until heated through. Remove from the heat, add the parsley, then toss the sauce through the pasta with the grated parmesan cheese.

NOTE: *Streaky bacon is the tail fatty ends of bacon rashers and adds flavour to the dish. You can use ordinary bacon slices if you prefer.*

NUTRITION PER SERVE
Protein 25 g; Fat 29 g; Carbohydrate 75 g; Dietary Fibre 7 g; Cholesterol 63 mg; 2745 kJ (655 Cal)

Cook the bacon until it is starting to brown, then add the tomato and cook until softened.

Add the cream and tomato pesto and stir until heated through.

Creamy pasta with peas and prosciutto

PREPARATION TIME: 15 MINUTES | TOTAL COOKING TIME: 20 MINUTES | SERVES 4

100 g (3½ oz) prosciutto, thinly sliced

3 teaspoons oil

2 eggs

250 ml (9 fl oz/1 cup) pouring (whipping) cream

35 g (1¼ oz/⅓ cup) finely grated parmesan cheese

2 tablespoons chopped flat-leaf (Italian) parsley

1 tablespoon snipped chives

250 g (9 oz) fresh or frozen peas

500 g (1 lb 2 oz) pasta shells or gnocchi

NUTRITION PER SERVE
Protein 21 g; Fat 32.5 g; Carbohydrate 41 g; Dietary Fibre 6 g; Cholesterol 201 mg; 2260 kJ (540 Cal)

1 Cut the prosciutto into thin strips. Heat the oil in a frying pan over medium heat, add the prosciutto and cook for 2 minutes, or until crisp. Drain on paper towels. Whisk together the eggs, cream, parmesan and herbs in a large bowl.

2 Bring a large saucepan of salted water to the boil. Add the peas and cook for 5 minutes, or until just tender. Leaving the pan on the heat, use a slotted spoon and transfer the peas to the bowl of cream mixture, and then add 3 tablespoons of the cooking liquid to the same bowl. Using a potato masher or the back of a fork, roughly mash the peas.

3 Add the pasta to the boiling water and cook until *al dente*. Drain well, then return to the pan. Add the cream mixture, then warm through over low heat, gently stirring for about 30 seconds until the pasta is coated in the sauce. Season to taste with salt and freshly ground black pepper. Divide among warmed plates, top with the prosciutto and serve immediately.

NOTE: *Be careful not to overheat or cook for too long or the egg will begin to scramble.*

Cut the prosciutto into thin strips and cook in the oil for 2 minutes, or until crisp.

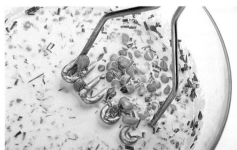
Add the cooked peas to the bowl of eggs, cream, parmesan and herbs and then roughly mash.

Cook the pasta until *al dente*, then add the cream sauce to the pan of drained pasta.

Rigatoni with chorizo and tomato

PREPARATION TIME: 15 MINUTES | TOTAL COOKING TIME: 25 MINUTES | SERVES 4

2 tablespoons olive oil
1 onion, sliced
250 g (9 oz) chorizo sausage, sliced
425 g (15 oz) tinned chopped tomatoes
125 ml (4 fl oz/½ cup) dry white wine
½–1 teaspoon chopped chilli, optional
375 g (13 oz) rigatoni
2 tablespoons chopped parsley, for serving
2 tablespoons grated parmesan cheese,
    for serving

1   Heat the oil in a frying pan. Add the onion and stir over low heat until tender.

2   Add the sliced sausage to the frying pan and cook, turning frequently, for 2–3 minutes. Add the tomato, wine and chilli and season with salt and pepper. Bring to the boil, reduce the heat and simmer for 15–20 minutes.

3   Meanwhile, cook the pasta in a large saucepan of rapidly boiling salted water until *al dente*. Drain well and return to the pan to keep warm. Add the sauce with half the combined parsley and parmesan cheese. Toss well. Serve sprinkled with the remaining combined parsley and parmesan, if desired.

VARIATION: *Use different hot sausage in place of chorizo.*

Add the sauce to the hot pasta and then add half the combined parsley and parmesan.

Add the chopped tomato, wine and chilli and season with salt and pepper.

NUTRITION PER SERVE
Protein 20 g; Fat 26 g; Carbohydrate 70 g; Dietary Fibre 6 g; Cholesterol 45 mg; 2578 kJ (616 Cal)

Farfalle with spinach and bacon

PREPARATION TIME: 10 MINUTES I TOTAL COOKING TIME: 15 MINUTES I SERVES 4

400 g (14 oz) farfalle
2 tablespoons extra virgin olive oil
250 g (9 oz) bacon slices, chopped
1 red onion, finely chopped
250 g (9 oz) baby English spinach leaves
1–2 tablespoons sweet chilli sauce
30 g (1 oz/¼ cup) crumbled feta cheese

1   Cook the pasta in a large saucepan of rapidly boiling salted water until *al dente*. Drain well and return to the pan to keep warm.

2   Meanwhile, heat the oil in a frying pan, add the bacon and cook over medium heat for 3 minutes, or until golden. Add the onion and cook for a further 4 minutes, or until softened. Toss the spinach leaves through the onion and bacon mixture for 30 seconds, or until the leaves are just wilted.

3   Add the bacon and spinach mixture to the drained pasta, then stir in the sweet chilli sauce. Season to taste with salt and freshly ground black pepper and toss well. Spoon into warm pasta bowls and scatter with the crumbled feta. Serve immediately.

NUTRITION PER SERVE
Protein 28 g; Fat 19 g; Carbohydrate 73 g; Dietary Fibre 7 g; Cholesterol 42 mg; 2415 kJ (575 Cal)

Cook the bacon over medium heat for 3 minutes or until golden.

Add the bacon and spinach mixture to the drained pasta and stir in the sweet chilli sauce.

Ziti with sausage

PREPARATION TIME: 10 MINUTES | TOTAL COOKING TIME: 35 MINUTES | SERVES 4

1 red capsicum (pepper)

1 green capsicum (pepper)

1 small eggplant (aubergine), sliced

3 tablespoons olive oil

1 onion, sliced

1 garlic clove, crushed

250 g (9 oz) chipolata sausages, sliced

425 g (15 oz) tinned chopped tomatoes

125 ml (4 fl oz/½ cup) red wine

3 tablespoons pitted black olives, halved

1 tablespoon chopped basil

1 tablespoon chopped parsley

500 g (1 lb 2 oz) ziti (see NOTE)

2 tablespoons grated parmesan cheese,
  for serving

1 Cut both capsicums into large flat pieces, removing the seeds and membranes. Place skin side up under a hot grill (broiler) until the skin blackens and blisters. Cool in a plastic bag then peel off the skin. Chop and set aside.

2 Brush the eggplant with a little oil. Grill (broil) until golden on each side, brushing with more oil as required. Set aside.

3 Heat the remaining oil in a frying pan. Add the onion and garlic and stir over low heat until the onion is tender. Add the chipolatas and cook until well browned.

4 Stir in the tomato, wine, olives, basil, parsley and season with salt and pepper. Bring to the boil. Reduce the heat and simmer for 15 minutes. Add the vegetables and heat through. Meanwhile, cook the ziti in a large saucepan of rapidly boiling salted water until *al dente*. Drain well and return to the pan to keep warm. Toss the vegetables and sauce through the pasta. Sprinkle with parmesan cheese before serving, if desired.

NOTE: *Ziti is a wide tubular pasta. You could use fettuccine or spaghetti.*

NUTRITION PER SERVE
Protein 19 g; Fat 19 g; Carbohydrate 97 g; Dietary Fibre 11 g; Cholesterol 5 mg; 2756 kJ (650 Cal)

Grill the capsicum to remove the skins and then chop the flesh.

Brush the eggplant with a little oil and grill until golden on both sides.

Cook the onion until it is tender and then add the sliced chipolatas.

Creamy veal and mushroom pasta

PREPARATION TIME: 15 MINUTES | TOTAL COOKING TIME: 30 MINUTES | SERVES 4

100 g (3½ oz) salted butter

500 g (1 lb 2 oz) veal schnitzel, cut into
   bite-sized pieces

300 g (10½ oz) Swiss brown mushrooms,
   sliced

3 garlic cloves, crushed

185 ml (6 fl oz/¾ cup) dry white wine

125 ml (4 fl oz/½ cup) chicken stock

200 ml (7 fl oz) thick (double/heavy) cream

1–2 tablespoons lemon juice

400 g (14 oz) pappardelle

1   Melt half the butter in a large frying pan over medium heat. Add the veal in batches and cook for 2–3 minutes, or until golden brown. Remove the veal from the pan and keep warm.

2   Add the remaining butter to the same frying pan and heat until foaming. Add the mushrooms and garlic and cook, stirring, over low heat for 5 minutes. Pour in the wine and stock, scraping the bottom of the pan with a wooden spoon, and simmer, covered, for 10 minutes.

3   Remove the lid, add the cream and simmer for 5 minutes, or until the sauce thickens. Stir in the lemon juice, veal and any juices until warmed through. Season to taste. Meanwhile, cook the pasta in a large saucepan of rapidly boiling salted water until *al dente*. Drain well, toss the sauce through the pasta and serve immediately.

Cook the veal in the butter in batches until it is golden brown.

Add the cream to the sauce and then simmer uncovered to allow it to thicken.

NUTRITION PER SERVE
Protein 45 g; Fat 41 g; Carbohydrate 74 g; Dietary
Fibre 5 g; Cholesterol 236 mg; 3660 kJ (875 Cal)

Pappardelle with salami, leek and provolone cheese

PREPARATION TIME: 15 MINUTES | TOTAL COOKING TIME: 15 MINUTES | SERVES 4

375 g (13 oz) pappardelle
2 tablespoons olive oil
2 leeks, thinly sliced (including some of
    the green section)
2 tablespoons dry white wine
800 g (1 lb 10 oz) tinned chopped tomatoes
150 g (5½ oz) sliced mild salami, cut into
    strips
2 small handfuls basil leaves, torn
125 g (4½ oz) provolone cheese, sliced
    into strips
30 g (1 oz) grated parmesan cheese, to serve

1   Cook the pasta in a large saucepan of rapidly boiling salted water until *al dente*. Drain well and return to the pan to keep warm. Meanwhile, heat the olive oil in a large deep frying pan, add the leek and cook over low heat for 4 minutes, or until soft but not browned. Increase the heat to medium, add the wine and stir until almost evaporated.

2   Add the tomato and salami, season with salt and freshly ground black pepper and simmer for 5 minutes, or until reduced slightly. Toss the tomato sauce mixture, basil and provolone lightly through the pasta. Sprinkle with parmesan and serve.

Cook the leek until it is soft but not browned and then add the wine.

Add the tomato and salami to the sauce and simmer until it has reduced a little.

NUTRITION PER SERVE
Protein 34 g; Fat 37 g; Carbohydrate 75 g; Dietary
Fibre 6 g; Cholesterol 94 mg; 3250 kJ (775 Cal)

Pasta with braised oxtail and celery

PREPARATION TIME: 20 MINUTES | TOTAL COOKING TIME: 3 HOURS 45 MINUTES | SERVES 4

1.5 kg (3 lb 5 oz) oxtail, jointed
3 tablespoons plain (all-purpose) flour, seasoned
3 tablespoons olive oil
1 onion, finely chopped
2 garlic cloves, crushed
500 ml (17 fl oz/2 cups) beef stock
425 g (15 oz) tin chopped tomatoes
250 ml (9 fl oz/1 cup) dry white wine
6 whole cloves
2 bay leaves
3 celery stalks, finely chopped
500 g (1 lb 2 oz) penne
30 g (1 oz) salted butter
3 tablespoons grated parmesan cheese

1 Preheat the oven to 160°C (315°F/ Gas 2–3). Dust the oxtail in the seasoned flour, shaking off any excess. Heat half the oil in a large frying pan and brown the oxtail over high heat in batches. Transfer the meat to a large ovenproof dish.

2 Wipe the frying pan clean with paper towels, add the remaining oil and the onion and garlic. Cook over low heat until the onion is tender. Stir in the stock, tomato, wine, cloves and bay leaves and season with salt and pepper. Bring to the boil and then pour over the oxtail.

3 Bake, covered, for 2½–3 hours. Add the celery and bake, uncovered, for another 30 minutes. Meanwhile, cook the pasta in a large saucepan of rapidly boiling salted water until *al dente.* Drain well and return to the pan to keep warm. Toss with the butter and parmesan. Serve the oxtail and sauce with the pasta.

HINT: *Seasoned flour is plain (all-purpose) flour to which seasonings of your choice have been added, for example: herbs, salt, pepper or dried mustard.*

NUTRITION PER SERVE
Protein 82 g; Fat 30 g; Carbohydrate 100 g; Dietary Fibre 8 g; Cholesterol 700 mg; 4388 kJ (1048 Cal)

Heat the oil in a large frying pan and brown the oxtail in batches.

Stir in the stock, tomato, wine, cloves and bay leaves and season to taste.

Bake the oxtail, covered, then add the celery and bake uncovered for a further 30 minutes.

Penne with bacon, ricotta and basil sauce

PREPARATION TIME: 20 MINUTES I TOTAL COOKING TIME: 15 MINUTES I SERVES 4

2 teaspoons olive oil
2 bacon slices, chopped
2–3 garlic cloves, crushed
1 onion, finely chopped
2 spring onions (scallions), finely chopped
250 g (9 oz/1 cup) ricotta cheese
1 very large handful finely chopped basil
325 g (11½ oz) penne
8 cherry tomatoes, halved

1 Heat the oil in a saucepan, add the bacon, garlic, onion and spring onion and stir over medium heat for 5 minutes, or until cooked. Remove from the heat, stir in the ricotta and chopped basil and beat until smooth.

2 Cook the pasta in a large saucepan of rapidly boiling salted water until *al dente*. Just prior to draining the pasta, add about 250 ml (9 fl oz/ 1 cup) of the pasta cooking water to the ricotta mixture to thin the sauce. Add more water if you prefer an even thinner sauce. Season with salt and pepper.

3 Drain the pasta and stir the sauce and tomato halves through the pasta. Garnish with small fresh basil leaves.

NUTRITION PER SERVE
Protein 20 g; Fat 10 g; Carbohydrate 65 g; Dietary Fibre 5 g; Cholesterol 40 mg; 1885 kJ (450 Cal)

Remove the bacon, garlic, onion and spring onion from the heat. Stir in the ricotta and basil.

Bring a large saucepan of salted water to a rapid boil before adding the pasta.

Thin the ricotta mixture with about a cup of the cooking water from the pasta.

Peppered pork and zucchini pasta

PREPARATION TIME: 15 MINUTES | TOTAL COOKING TIME: 25 MINUTES | SERVES 4

450 g (1 lb) pork fillet

3–4 teaspoons cracked black peppercorns

90 g (3¼ oz) butter

250 g (9 oz) pasta

1 onion, halved and thinly sliced

2 large zucchini (courgettes), thinly sliced

1 large handful basil, torn

150 g (5½ oz/¾ cup) baby black olives

60 g (2¼ oz/½ cup) grated romano cheese

1 Cut the pork fillet in half widthways and roll in the cracked peppercorns and some salt. Heat half the butter in a large deep frying pan, add the pork and cook for 4 minutes on each side, or until golden brown and just cooked through. Remove from the pan and cut into thin slices, then set aside and keep warm.

2 Cook the pasta in a large saucepan of rapidly boiling salted water until *al dente*. Drain well and return to the pan to keep warm. Meanwhile, melt the remaining butter in the frying pan, add the onion and cook, stirring, over medium heat for about 3 minutes, or until soft. Add the zucchini and toss for 5 minutes, or until starting to soften. Add the basil, olives, sliced pork and any juices and toss well. Stir the pork mixture through the hot pasta, then season well. Serve immediately, topped with the romano cheese.

Fry the pork in butter until it is golden brown and just cooked through, then cut into thin slices.

Toss together the onion, zucchini, basil, olives, pork and any juices.

NUTRITION PER SERVE
Protein 39 g; Fat 22 g; Carbohydrate 53 g; Dietary Fibre 5 g; Cholesterol 114 mg; 2340 kJ (560 Cal)

Pasta
with chicken

Creamy rigatoni with chicken and tomato sauce

PREPARATION TIME: 15 MINUTES | TOTAL COOKING TIME: 20 MINUTES | SERVES 4–6

500 g (1 lb 2 oz) rigatoni

1 tablespoon olive oil

4 boneless, skinless chicken breasts, thinly sliced

4 ripe tomatoes, diced

150 g (5½ oz/1 cup) sun-dried tomatoes in oil, thinly sliced

2 tablespoons sun-dried tomato paste (concentrated purée) (see NOTE)

1 handful small basil leaves

300 ml (10½ fl oz) pouring (whipping) cream

200 ml (7 fl oz) chicken stock

1 Cook the pasta in a large saucepan of rapidly boiling salted water until *al dente.* Drain well and return to the pan to keep warm.

2 Meanwhile, heat the oil in a deep frying pan and cook the chicken over high heat for 1–1½ minutes on each side, or until browned and cooked through. Remove from the pan and keep warm.

3 Return the frying pan to the heat and add the tomato, sun-dried tomato, tomato paste and half the basil leaves. Cook over medium heat for 5 minutes, or until the tomato starts to soften. Stir in the cream and chicken stock and bring to the boil, stirring constantly.

4 Reduce the heat and return the chicken to the pan. Add the warm rigatoni and season with pepper. Heat gently until the chicken and pasta are warmed through. Top with the remaining basil leaves and serve immediately.

NOTE: *Sun-dried tomato paste is available in good supermarkets. Or, you can make your own by processing whole sun-dried tomatoes in oil with a little of their oil until a smooth paste is formed.*

NUTRITION PER SERVE (6)
Protein 45 g; Fat 50 g; Carbohydrate 90 g; Dietary Fibre 8 g; Cholesterol 195 mg; 4227 kJ (1010 Cal)

Cook the chicken over high heat until browned and cooked through.

Cook the tomato, sun-dried tomato, tomato paste and half the basil.

Return the chicken to the pan and toss through the rigatoni.

Penne with chicken and mushrooms

PREPARATION TIME: 15 MINUTES | TOTAL COOKING TIME: 25 MINUTES | SERVES 4

30 g (1 oz) salted butter
1 tablespoon olive oil
1 onion, sliced
1 garlic clove, crushed
60 g (2¼ oz) prosciutto, chopped
250 g (9 oz) boneless, skinless chicken thighs, trimmed and sliced
125 g (4½ oz) button mushrooms, sliced
1 tomato, peeled, halved and sliced
1 tablespoon tomato paste (concentrated purée)
125 ml (4 fl oz/½ cup) white wine
250 ml (9 fl oz/1 cup) pouring (whipping) cream
500 g (1 lb 2 oz) penne
2 tablespoons grated parmesan cheese, for serving

1 Heat the butter and oil in a large frying pan. Add the onion and garlic and stir over low heat until the onion is tender. Add the prosciutto and fry until crisp.

2 Add the chicken and cook over medium heat for 3 minutes. Add the mushrooms and cook for another 2 minutes. Stir in the tomato and tomato paste and then the wine. Bring to the boil. Reduce the heat and simmer until reduced by half.

3 Stir in the cream and season with salt and pepper. Bring to the boil. Reduce the heat again and simmer until the sauce begins to thicken. Meanwhile, cook the pasta in a large saucepan of rapidly boiling salted water until *al dente*. Drain well and return to pan. Add the sauce and toss to combine. Serve immediately, sprinkled with the parmesan, if desired.

HINT: *You can use minced (ground) chicken in this recipe instead of sliced chicken thighs.*

NUTRITION PER SERVE
Protein 23 g; Fat 60 g; Carbohydrate 14 g; Dietary Fibre 3 g; Cholesterol 255 mg; 2888 kJ (700 Cal)

Fry the onion and garlic in the butter and oil until the onion is tender.

Add the tomato and tomato paste and stir in, then add the wine.

Chicken and eggplant pasta

PREPARATION TIME: 15 MINUTES | TOTAL COOKING TIME: 15 MINUTES | SERVES 4

375 g (13 oz) penne

100 ml (3½ fl oz) olive oil

4 slender eggplants (aubergines), thinly sliced on the diagonal

2 boneless, skinless chicken breasts

2 teaspoons lemon juice

1 large handful flat-leaf (Italian) parsley, chopped

270 g (9½ oz) chargrilled red capsicum (pepper), drained and sliced (see NOTE)

150 g (5½ oz) fresh asparagus, trimmed, blanched and cut into short lengths

90 g (3¼ oz) semi-dried (sun-blushed) tomatoes, finely sliced

parmesan cheese, shaved, to serve

1 Cook the pasta in a large saucepan of rapidly boiling salted water until *al dente*. Drain well and return to the pan to keep warm. Meanwhile, heat 2 tablespoons of the oil in a large frying pan over high heat and cook the eggplant for 4–5 minutes, or until golden and cooked through.

2 Heat a lightly oiled chargrill pan over high heat and cook the chicken for 5 minutes each side, or until browned and cooked through. Cut into thick slices. Combine the lemon juice, parsley and the remaining oil in a small screw-top jar and shake well. Return the pasta to the heat, toss through the dressing, chicken, eggplant, capsicum, asparagus and tomato until well mixed and warmed through. Season with black pepper. Serve warm with a little shaved parmesan.

NOTE: *You can buy jars of chargrilled capsicum at the supermarket; otherwise, visit your local deli.*

Fry the eggplant in a large frying pan until golden and cooked through.

Chargrill the chicken breasts until browned and cooked through on both sides.

NUTRITION PER SERVE
Protein 50 g; Fat 28 g; Carbohydrate 72 g; Dietary Fibre 7.5 g; Cholesterol 114 mg; 3120 kJ (745 Cal)

Spaghetti with chicken meatballs

PREPARATION TIME: 30 MINUTES + CHILLING | TOTAL COOKING TIME: 1 HOUR 30 MINUTES | SERVES 4–6

500 g (1 lb 2 oz) minced (ground) chicken

60 g (2¼ oz) grated parmesan cheese, plus extra, to serve

160 g (5⅔ oz/2 cups) fresh white breadcrumbs

2 garlic cloves, crushed

1 egg

1 tablespoon chopped flat-leaf (Italian) parsley

1 tablespoon chopped sage

3 tablespoons vegetable oil

500 g (1 lb 2 oz) spaghetti

2 tablespoons chopped oregano, to serve

TOMATO SAUCE

1 tablespoon olive oil

1 onion, finely chopped

2 kg (4 lb 8 oz) ripe tomatoes, roughly chopped

2 bay leaves

1 very large handful basil leaves

1 teaspoon coarse ground black pepper

1 In a large bowl, mix together the mince, parmesan, breadcrumbs, garlic, egg, pepper and herbs. Shape tablespoons of the mixture into small balls and refrigerate for 30 minutes to firm. Heat the oil in a shallow frying pan and fry the balls in batches until golden brown; turn often by shaking the pan. Remove and drain on paper towels.

2 To make the tomato sauce, heat the oil in a large saucepan, add the onion and fry for 1–2 minutes. Add the tomato and bay leaves, cover and bring to the boil, stirring occasionally. Reduce the heat to low, partially cover and cook for 50–60 minutes.

3 Add the meatballs, basil leaves and pepper and simmer for 10–15 minutes, uncovered. Meanwhile, cook the spaghetti in a large saucepan of rapidly boiling salted water until *al dente*. Drain well and return to the pan. Add some sauce to the pasta and toss. Serve the pasta in individual bowls with sauce and meatballs, sprinkled with fresh oregano and a little extra parmesan cheese, if desired.

NUTRITION PER SERVE (6)
Protein 30 g; Fat 23 g; Carbohydrate 86 g; Dietary Fibre 10 g; Cholesterol 60 mg; 2876 kJ (690 Cal)

Shape tablespoons of the mixture into small balls and refrigerate for 30 minutes to firm up.

Add the meatballs, basil and pepper to the tomato mixture and simmer, uncovered, for 10 minutes.

Penne with chicken, asparagus and goat's cheese

PREPARATION TIME: 15 MINUTES I TOTAL COOKING TIME: 35 MINUTES I SERVES 4

500 g (1 lb 2 oz) penne
350 g (12 oz) asparagus spears
1 tablespoon olive oil
2 boneless, skinless chicken breasts, cut into
    small cubes
1 tablespoon finely chopped thyme
250 ml (9 fl oz/1 cup) chicken stock
4 tablespoons balsamic vinegar
150 g (5½ oz/1¼ cups) goat's cheese,
    crumbled

1   Cook the pasta in a large saucepan of rapidly boiling salted water until *al dente.* Drain well and return to the pan to keep warm.

2   Remove the woody ends from the asparagus, cut into short lengths and cook in a saucepan of boiling water for 3 minutes, or until just tender.

3   Heat the oil in a saucepan over high heat. Add the chicken and cook in batches, stirring occasionally, for 5 minutes, or until browned. Return all the chicken to the pan. Add the thyme and cook for 1 minute. Add the stock and vinegar and bring to the boil. Reduce the heat and simmer, stirring, for 3–4 minutes, or until the sauce has reduced slightly, then add the asparagus. Toss the pasta with the chicken in a serving bowl and sprinkle with the cheese. Season and serve.

VARIATION: *You can use feta instead of goat's cheese.*

The woody ends of the asparagus will snap off easily when you gently bend the stalk.

Simmer the sauce for a few minutes to reduce it slightly before adding the asparagus.

NUTRITION PER SERVE
Protein 45 g; Fat 17 g; Carbohydrate 90 g; Dietary Fibre 7.5 g; Cholesterol 75 mg; 2957 kJ (705 Cal)

Smoked chicken linguine

PREPARATION TIME: 15 MINUTES | TOTAL COOKING TIME: 20 MINUTES | SERVES 4

1 tablespoon olive oil

1 leek, thinly sliced

3 large garlic cloves, finely chopped

125 ml (4 fl oz/½ cup) dry white wine

300 g (10½ oz) Swiss brown mushrooms, sliced

2 teaspoons chopped thyme

300 ml (10½ fl oz) thickened (whipping) cream

2 smoked boneless, skinless chicken breasts, thinly sliced (see NOTE)

350 g (12 oz) fresh linguine

1 Heat the oil in a saucepan. Add the leek and cook, stirring, over low heat for 3–4 minutes, or until soft. Add the garlic and cook for another minute. Pour in the wine and simmer for 2–3 minutes, or until the liquid has reduced by half.

2 Increase the heat to medium, add the mushrooms and thyme and cook for 5 minutes, or until any excess liquid has been absorbed, then add the cream and sliced chicken. Reduce the heat and simmer for 4–5 minutes, or until the sauce has slightly thickened.

3 Meanwhile, cook the pasta in a large saucepan of rapidly boiling salted water until *al dente*. Drain and divide among serving plates. Spoon on the sauce and serve.

NOTE: *Buy smoked chicken at the deli section of good supermarkets.*

Cook the leek in the oil for 3–4 minutes, or until it is soft.

Add the cream and chicken and simmer until the sauce has slightly thickened.

NUTRITION PER SERVE
Protein 33 g; Fat 40 g; Carbohydrate 53 g; Dietary Fibre 4 g; Cholesterol 207 mg; 2990 kJ (715 Cal)

Warm minted chicken pasta

PREPARATION TIME: 15 MINUTES I TOTAL COOKING TIME: 20 MINUTES I SERVES 4

250 g (9 oz) pasta
125 ml (4 fl oz/½ cup) olive oil
1 large red capsicum (pepper)
3 boneless, skinless chicken breasts
6 spring onions (scallions), cut into short
    lengths
4 garlic cloves, thinly sliced
2 large handfuls chopped mint
4 tablespoons cider vinegar
100 g (3½ oz) baby English spinach

NUTRITION PER SERVE
Protein 47 g; Fat 30 g; Carbohydrate 47g; Dietary
Fibre 6 g; Cholesterol 84 mg; 2705 kJ (645 Cal)

1   Cook the pasta in a large saucepan of
rapidly boiling salted water until *al dente*.
Drain well, return to the pan to keep warm
and toss with a tablespoon of the oil.

2   Meanwhile, cut the capsicum into
quarters, removing the seeds and membrane.
Place, skin side up, under a hot grill (broiler)
for 8–10 minutes, or until the skin blackens and
blisters. Cool in a plastic bag, then peel away
the skin. Cut into thin strips. Place the chicken
breast between two sheets of plastic wrap
and press with the palm of your hand until
slightly flattened.

3   Heat another tablespoon of the oil in a
large frying pan, add the chicken and cook over
medium heat for 5 minutes on each side, or
until light brown and cooked through. Remove
from the pan and cut into thin slices.

4   Add another tablespoon of the oil to the
pan and add the spring onion, garlic and
capsicum. Cook, stirring, for 2–3 minutes, or
until starting to soften. Add most of the mint,
the vinegar and the remaining oil and stir until
warmed through. Toss together the pasta,
chicken, spinach, onion mixture and remaining
mint. Serve warm.

Place the chicken between two sheets of plastic
wrap and flatten slightly with your hand.

Brown the chicken until cooked through and then
cut into slices.

Pasta with artichokes and chargrilled chicken

PREPARATION TIME: 10 MINUTES I TOTAL COOKING TIME: 30 MINUTES I SERVES 6

1 tablespoon olive oil

3 boneless, skinless chicken breasts

500 g (1 lb 2 oz) pasta

8 prosciutto slices

280 g (10 oz) jar artichokes in oil, drained and quartered, oil reserved

150 g (5½ oz) semi-dried (sun-blushed) tomatoes, thinly sliced

90 g (3¼ oz) baby rocket (arugula) leaves

2–3 tablespoons balsamic vinegar

1 Lightly brush a chargrill or frying pan with the oil and heat over high heat. Cook the chicken for 5–6 minutes on each side, or until cooked through. Thinly slice and set aside.

2 Cook the pasta in a large saucepan of rapidly boiling salted water until *al dente*. Drain well and return to the pan to keep warm. Meanwhile, place the prosciutto on a grill tray and cook under a hot grill (broiler) for 2 minutes on each side, or until crisp. Cool slightly and break into pieces. Combine the pasta with the chicken, prosciutto, artichokes, tomato and rocket in a bowl and toss. Whisk together 3 tablespoons of the reserved artichoke oil and the balsamic vinegar and toss through the pasta mixture. Season and serve.

You can either fry or chargrill the chicken breasts, then thinly slice.

Cook the prosciutto under a hot grill until crisp. Allow to cool, then break into pieces.

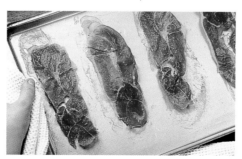

NUTRITION PER SERVE
Protein 30 g; Fat 9 g; Carbohydrate 51 g; Dietary Fibre 4 g; Cholesterol 103 mg; 1705 kJ (410 Cal)

Creamy chicken and peppercorn pappardelle

PREPARATION TIME: 15 MINUTES | TOTAL COOKING TIME: 15 MINUTES | SERVES 4

2 boneless, skinless chicken breasts
30 g (1 oz) salted butter
1 onion, halved and thinly sliced
2 tablespoons drained green peppercorns,
　slightly crushed
125 ml (4 fl oz/¼ cup) dry white wine
300 ml (10½ fl oz) pouring (whipping) cream
400 g (14 oz) pappardelle
90 g (3¼ oz) sour cream (optional)
2 tablespoons snipped chives

1　Cut the chicken in half so that you have four flat breasts and season with salt and pepper. Melt the butter in a frying pan, add the chicken and cook for 3 minutes on each side, or until lightly browned and cooked through. Remove from the pan, cut into slices and keep warm.

2　Add the onion and peppercorns to the same pan and cook over medium heat for 3 minutes, or until the onion has softened slightly. Add the wine and cook for 1 minute, or until reduced by half. Stir in the cream and cook for 4–5 minutes, or until thickened slightly, then season with salt and pepper.

3　Meanwhile, cook the pasta in a large saucepan of rapidly boiling salted water until *al dente*. Drain well and return to the pan to keep warm. Mix together the pasta, chicken with any juices and cream sauce. Divide the pasta among serving bowls, top with a dollop of sour cream (if using) and sprinkle with chives.

Cut the chicken in half to make four flat breasts that will cook through quickly.

Stir in the cream and cook for 4-5 minutes, or until the sauce thickens slightly.

NUTRITION PER SERVE
Protein 38 g; Fat 50 g; Carbohydrate 60 g; Dietary Fibre 1.5 g; Cholesterol 250 mg; 3580 kJ (855 Cal)

Tagliatelle with chicken livers and cream

PREPARATION TIME: 20 MINUTES | TOTAL COOKING TIME: 15 MINUTES | SERVES 4

2 tablespoons olive oil

1 onion, finely chopped

1 garlic clove, crushed

300 g (10½ oz) chicken livers, chopped into small pieces

250 ml (9 fl oz/1 cup) pouring (whipping) cream

1 tablespoon snipped chives

1 teaspoon wholegrain mustard

2 eggs, beaten

375 g (13 oz) tagliatelle

2 tablespoons grated parmesan cheese, for serving

1   Heat the oil in a large frying pan. Add the onion and garlic and stir over low heat until the onion is tender. Add the chicken livers to the pan and cook gently for 2–3 minutes. Remove from the heat.

2   Stir in the cream, chives and mustard and season with salt and pepper. Return to the heat and bring the sauce to the boil. Add the eggs, stirring gently. Remove from the heat.

3   Meanwhile, cook the pasta in a large saucepan of rapidly boiling salted water until *al dente*. Drain well and return to the pan to keep warm. Add the sauce and toss well to combine. Serve in warmed pasta bowls with grated parmesan, if desired.

NUTRITION PER SERVE
Protein 25 g; Fat 35 g; Carbohydrate 70 g; Dietary Fibre 5 g; Cholesterol 70 mg; 2914 kJ (700 Cal)

Trim any fat or gristle from the chicken livers before cutting them into small pieces.

Cook the onion and garlic until the onion is tender and then add the livers.

Add the beaten eggs to the sauce, stirring to combine, then remove quickly from the heat.

Pasta
with seafood

Saffron pasta with garlic prawns and preserved lemon

PREPARATION TIME: 20 MINUTES | TOTAL COOKING TIME: 20 MINUTES | SERVES 4

125 ml (4 fl oz/½ cup) dry white wine
pinch of saffron threads
500 g (1 lb 2 oz) fresh saffron or plain
    angel hair pasta
1 tablespoon virgin olive oil
30 g (1 oz) salted butter
750 g (1 lb 10 oz) raw prawns (shrimp),
    peeled and deveined, leaving tails intact
3 garlic cloves, crushed
100 g (3½ oz) butter, for pan-frying, extra
½ preserved lemon, rinsed, pith and flesh
    removed, cut into thin strips
1 tablespoon lemon juice
4 spring onions (scallions), thinly sliced
4 makrut (kaffir lime) leaves, thinly shredded
125 ml (4 fl oz/½ cup) chicken stock
2 tablespoons snipped chives

NUTRITION PER SERVE
Protein 15 g; Fat 27 g; Carbohydrate 90 g; Dietary
Fibre 7.5 g; Cholesterol 64 mg; 2888 kJ (690 Cal)

1   Place the wine and saffron threads in a small saucepan and boil for 3 minutes, or until reduced by half. Remove from the heat.

2   Cook the pasta in a large saucepan of rapidly boiling salted water until *al dente*. Drain well and return to the pan to keep warm.

3   Heat the oil and butter in a large frying pan and cook the prawns in batches over high heat for 3 minutes, or until pink and tender. Cut into thirds, then transfer to a plate and keep warm.

4   Add the garlic and extra butter to the same pan and cook over medium heat for 3 minutes, or until golden. Add the wine and stir to remove any sediment from the bottom of the pan. Add the preserved lemon, lemon juice, spring onion, makrut leaves and stock and bring to the boil, then reduce the heat and simmer for 2 minutes.

5   Return the prawns to the frying pan and heat through. Serve the pasta topped with some of the prawns and the preserved lemon sauce and sprinkle with chives.

Cook the pasta in a large saucepan until *al dente*, then drain well.

Cook the prawns in batches until they are pink and tender.

Add the wine and stir well to incorporate any bits that are sticking to the bottom of the pan.

Angel hair pasta with garlic, scallops and rocket

PREPARATION TIME: 10 MINUTES I TOTAL COOKING TIME: 15 MINUTES I SERVES 4

20 large scallops with roe
250 g (9 oz) angel hair pasta
150 ml (5 fl oz) extra virgin olive oil
2 garlic cloves, finely chopped
3 tablespoons dry white wine
1 tablespoon lemon juice
100 g (3½ oz) baby rocket (arugula) leaves
2 large handfuls chopped coriander (cilantro) leaves

1 Pull or trim any veins, membrane or hard white muscle from the scallops. Pat the scallops dry with paper towels. Cook the pasta in a large saucepan of rapidly boiling salted water until *al dente*. Drain well and transfer to a bowl. Toss with 1 tablespoon of the oil.

2 Meanwhile, heat 1 tablespoon of the oil in a frying pan, add the garlic and cook for a few seconds, or until fragrant. Do not brown. Add the wine and lemon juice, and remove from the heat.

3 Heat a chargrill pan or barbecue grill plate over high heat and brush with a little oil. Season the scallops with salt and pepper and cook for 1 minute on each side, or until just cooked. Gently reheat the garlic mixture, add the rocket and stir over medium heat for 1–2 minutes, or until wilted. Toss through the pasta and mix together well. Add the remaining oil and half the coriander and mix well. Divide the pasta among four bowls, arrange the scallops over the top and garnish with the remaining coriander.

VARIATION: *Add ½ teaspoon dried chilli flakes just before the wine and lemon juice for an added kick.*

Transfer the pasta to a bowl to cool and toss with a little oil.

You can cook the scallops on a chargrill pan or barbecue plate.

NUTRITION PER SERVE
Protein 15 g; Fat 37 g; Carbohydrate 45 g; Dietary Fibre 4 g; Cholesterol 20 mg; 2425 kJ (580 Cal)

Smoked salmon pasta

PREPARATION TIME: 10 MINUTES | TOTAL COOKING TIME: 15 MINUTES | SERVES 4

500 g (1 lb 2 oz) pasta
1 tablespoon olive oil
4 spring onions (scallions), finely chopped
180 g (6¼ oz/2 cups) button mushrooms, sliced
250 ml (9 fl oz/1 cup) dry white wine
300 ml (10½ fl oz) pouring (whipping) cream
1 tablespoon finely chopped dill
1 tablespoon lemon juice
90 g (3¼ oz) parmesan cheese, grated
200 g (7 oz) smoked salmon, cut into strips
shaved parmesan and lemon wedges, to serve

1 Cook the pasta in a large saucepan of rapidly boiling salted water until *al dente*. Drain well and return to the pan to keep warm.

2 Meanwhile, heat the oil in a small saucepan, add the spring onion and mushrooms and cook over medium heat for 1–2 minutes, or until soft. Add the wine and cream and bring to the boil, then reduce the heat and simmer for 1 minute.

3 Pour the mushroom sauce over the pasta and stir through the dill and lemon juice. Add the parmesan and stir. Remove from the heat and stir in the smoked salmon. Season with pepper and serve with parmesan shavings and lemon wedges.

NUTRITION PER SERVE
Protein 40 g; Fat 60 g; Carbohydrate 90 g; Dietary Fibre 8 g; Cholesterol 184 mg; 4608 kJ (1101 Cal)

Cook the spring onion and mushrooms over medium heat until soft.

Add the wine and cream to the saucepan and bring to the boil.

Tuna and chermoula on pappardelle

PREPARATION TIME: 15 MINUTES + 20 MINUTES MARINATING | TOTAL COOKING TIME: 30 MINUTES | SERVES 4

500 g (1 lb 2 oz) sweet potato, cut into small cubes

100 ml (3½ fl oz) olive oil

2 large handfuls coriander (cilantro) leaves, finely chopped

2 very large handfuls flat-leaf (Italian) parsley, chopped

3 garlic cloves, crushed

3 teaspoons ground cumin

¾ teaspoon cracked black pepper

3 tablespoons lemon juice

4 x 180 g (6¼ oz) tuna steaks

400 g (14 oz) pappardelle

NUTRITION PER SERVE
Protein 62 g; Fat 34 g; Carbohydrate 90 g; Dietary Fibre 7 g; Cholesterol 83 mg; 3830 kJ (915 Cal)

1 Preheat the oven to 200°C (400°F/Gas 6). Toss the sweet potato in 2 tablespoons of the oil, place on a baking tray and roast for 25–30 minutes, or until tender.

2 To make the chermoula, place the coriander, parsley, garlic, cumin and cracked black pepper in a small food processor and process to a rough paste. Transfer to a bowl and stir in the lemon juice and 1 tablespoon of the oil. Place the tuna in a non-metallic bowl, cover with 2 tablespoons of the chermoula and toss until it is evenly coated. Marinate in the refrigerator for 20 minutes. Meanwhile, cook the pasta in a large saucepan of rapidly boiling salted water until *al dente*. Drain well and return to the pan to keep warm. Toss with the remaining chermoula and oil.

3 Heat a lightly oiled chargrill pan over high heat. Cook the tuna for 2 minutes on each side, or until cooked to your liking. Cut into small cubes, toss through the pasta with the sweet potato and serve.

Toss the sweet potato in 2 tablespoons of oil and roast until tender.

Process the coriander, parsley, garlic, cumin and black pepper, then add the lemon juice and oil.

Cook the tuna for a couple of minutes on each side on a lightly oiled chargrill pan.

Pappardelle with lobster and saffron cream sauce

PREPARATION TIME: 10 MINUTES I TOTAL COOKING TIME: 20 MINUTES I SERVES 4–6

400 g (14 oz) pappardelle
60 g (2¼ oz) salted butter
4 large garlic cloves, crushed
250 g (9 oz) Swiss brown mushrooms, sliced
500 g (1 lb 2 oz) fresh or frozen lobster tail
    meat or raw bug tails, cut into chunks
125 ml (4 fl oz/½ cup) dry white wine
½ teaspoon saffron threads
700 ml (24 fl oz) thickened (whipping) cream
2 egg yolks

1 Cook the pasta in a large saucepan of rapidly boiling salted water until *al dente*. Drain well and return to the pan to keep warm. Meanwhile, melt the butter in a large deep frying pan, add the garlic and mushrooms and cook over medium heat for 2–3 minutes, or until soft. Add the lobster (or bug) and cook for 4–5 minutes, or until just cooked through. Remove from the pan.

2 Add the wine and saffron to the pan, scraping the bottom to collect any bits. Bring to the boil and cook for 2–3 minutes, or until reduced. Add the cream, reduce the heat and simmer for 5 minutes. Whisk through the egg yolks until thickened. Return the lobster mixture to the pan and stir until warmed through. Drain the pasta and divide among serving dishes. Spoon on the lobster sauce and season to taste. Serve immediately.

Cook the garlic and mushrooms until soft then add the lobster meat.

Add the cream to the sauce, then reduce the heat and simmer to thicken.

NUTRITION PER SERVE (6)
Protein 29 g; Fat 55 g; Carbohydrate 52 g; Dietary Fibre 3 g; Cholesterol 309 mg; 3430 kJ (820 Cal)

Spaghetti with shellfish and white wine sauce

PREPARATION TIME: 15 MINUTES | TOTAL COOKING TIME: 15 MINUTES | SERVES 4

500 g (1 lb 2 oz) mussels

1 kg (2 lb 4 oz) clams (vongole)

400 g (14 oz) spaghetti

2 tablespoons olive oil

4 French shallots (eschalots), finely chopped

2 garlic cloves, crushed

250 ml (9 fl oz/1 cup) dry white wine

3 tablespoons chopped flat-leaf (Italian) parsley

1   Scrub the mussels with a stiff brush and remove any barnacles with a knife. Pull away the hairy beards. Discard any mussels or clams that are broken or open ones that do not close when tapped on the work surface. Wash them all thoroughly under cold running water. Cook the pasta in a large saucepan of rapidly boiling salted water until *al dente*. Drain well and return to the pan to keep warm.

2   Meanwhile, heat the oil in a large saucepan over medium heat and cook the shallots for 4 minutes, or until softened. Add the garlic and cook for a further 1 minute. Pour in the wine, bring to the boil and cook for 2 minutes, or until reduced slightly. Add the clams and mussels, tossing to coat them in the liquid, then cover the pan. Cook, shaking the pan regularly, for about 3 minutes, or until the shells have opened. Discard any clams or mussels that do not open in the cooking time. Toss the clam mixture through the spaghetti, scatter with parsley and transfer to a warmed serving dish. Season and serve with salad and bread.

Scrub the mussels and then pull away the hairy beards that grow between the shells.

Cook the mussels and clams in the sauce for 3 minutes, discarding any that don't open.

Crab, camembert and fusilli frittata

PREPARATION TIME: 15 MINUTES | TOTAL COOKING TIME: 50 MINUTES | SERVES 4–6

90 g (3¼ oz/1 cup) fusilli

1 tablespoon olive oil

1 very small red onion, finely chopped

1 large roma (plum) tomato, roughly chopped

60 g (2¼ oz) semi-dried (sun-blushed) tomatoes, roughly chopped

2 tablespoons finely chopped coriander (cilantro) leaves

150 g (5½ oz/⅔ cup) cooked fresh or tinned crabmeat

150 g (5½ oz) camembert cheese, rind removed, cut into small pieces

6 eggs, plus 2 egg yolks

> NUTRITION PER SERVE (6)
> Protein 19 g; Fat 17 g; Carbohydrate 13 g; Dietary Fibre 2 g; Cholesterol 293 mg; 1155 kJ (275 Cal)

1 Cook the pasta in a large saucepan of rapidly boiling salted water until *al dente*. Drain well and set aside to cool a little.

2 Meanwhile, heat half the oil in a small frying pan over low heat, add the onion and cook for 4–5 minutes, or until softened but not browned. Transfer to a bowl and add the roma tomato, semi-dried tomato and coriander. Squeeze out any excess moisture from the crabmeat and add to the bowl. Add half the cheese and the cooled pasta. Mix well. Beat together the 6 eggs and the 2 extra yolks, then stir into the frittata mixture. Season with salt and pepper.

3 Heat the remaining oil in the frying pan, pour in the frittata mixture and cook over low heat for 25 minutes. Preheat the grill (broiler) to low. Scatter the remaining camembert over the frittata before placing it under the grill for 10–15 minutes, or until cooked and golden brown on top. Remove from the grill and leave for 5 minutes. Cut into slices to serve.

Add the cooked pasta to the mixture and then the eggs.

Cook the frittata over low heat for 25 minutes and then place under the grill to brown.

Spaghetti with tuna, basil and capers

PREPARATION TIME: 10 MINUTES | TOTAL COOKING TIME: 15 MINUTES | SERVES 4

500 g (1 lb 2 oz) spaghetti
1 tablespoon extra virgin olive oil
2 garlic cloves, crushed
250 g (9 oz) tinned tuna in brine, drained and
    broken into chunks
2 very large handfuls basil leaves, torn
4 vine-ripened tomatoes, roughly chopped
2 tablespoons capers, drained and rinsed,
    roughly chopped
90 g (3¼ oz) parmesan cheese, grated

1   Cook the pasta in a large saucepan of rapidly boiling salted water until *al dente*. Drain well and return to the pan to keep warm.

2   Meanwhile, heat the oil in a small saucepan, add the garlic and tuna and cook over medium heat for 1 minute, or until the garlic is fragrant and the tuna is warmed through.

3   Add the tuna mixture, basil, tomato, capers and parmesan to the spaghetti and mix together well. Season and serve with crusty bread.

NUTRITION PER SERVE
Protein 48 g; Fat 20 g; Carbohydrate 93 g; Dietary Fibre 9.5 g; Cholesterol 60 mg; 3147 kJ (752 Cal)

Using a sharp knife, roughly chop the vine-ripened tomatoes.

Cook the garlic and tuna over medium heat for 1 minute.

Mix together the spaghetti, tuna, basil, tomato, capers and parmesan.

Salmon and pasta mornay

PREPARATION TIME: **10** MINUTES | TOTAL COOKING TIME: **15** MINUTES | SERVES **4**

400 g (14 oz) small shell pasta

30 g (1 oz) salted butter

6 spring onions (scallions), chopped

2 garlic cloves, crushed

1 tablespoon plain (all-purpose) flour

250 ml (9 fl oz/1 cup) milk

250 g (9 oz/1 cup) sour cream

1 tablespoon lemon juice

425 g (15 oz) tinned salmon, drained and
    flaked

1 large handful chopped parsley

1   Cook the pasta in a large saucepan of rapidly boiling salted water until *al dente*. Drain well and return to the pan to keep warm.

2   Meanwhile, melt the butter in a saucepan and cook the spring onion and garlic over low heat for 3 minutes or until soft. Add the flour and stir for 1 minute. Mix together the milk, sour cream and lemon juice and slowly add to the pan, stirring constantly. Stir over medium heat for 3 minutes or until the sauce boils and thickens.

3   Add the salmon and parsley to the sauce and stir for 1 minute to heat through. Toss with the pasta and season before serving.

STORAGE: *The sauce can be kept for up to a day, covered in the refrigerator. Cook the pasta and reheat the sauce just before serving.*

VARIATION: *Use tinned tuna instead of salmon. Add 1 teaspoon of mustard to the sauce.*

Combine the milk, sour cream and lemon juice and stir slowly into the sauce.

Once the sauce is cooked, add the drained pasta to the pan and toss well.

NUTRITION PER SERVE
Protein 39 g; Fat 42 g; Carbohydrate 78 g; Dietary Fibre 6 g; Cholesterol 192 mg; 3530 kJ (852 Cal)

Tagliatelle with octopus

PREPARATION TIME: 15 MINUTES | TOTAL COOKING TIME: 20 MINUTES | SERVES 4

500 g (1 lb 2 oz) tagliatelle

2 tablespoons olive oil

1 onion, sliced

1 garlic clove, crushed

425 g (15 oz) tinned chopped tomatoes

125 ml (4 fl oz/½ cup) dry white wine

1 tablespoon chilli sauce

1 tablespoon chopped basil

1 kg (2 lb 4 oz) baby octopus, cleaned and halved (see NOTE)

NUTRITION PER SERVE
Protein 58 g; Fat 14 g; Carbohydrate 96 g; Dietary
Fibre 9 g; Cholesterol 50 mg; 3230 kJ (772 Cal)

---

1   Cook the pasta in a large saucepan of rapidly boiling salted water until *al dente.* Drain well and return to the pan to keep warm.

2   Meanwhile, heat the oil in a large frying pan. Add the onion and garlic and stir over low heat until the onion is tender. Add the tomato, wine, chilli sauce, basil and season with salt and pepper. Bring to the boil. Reduce the heat and simmer for 10 minutes.

3   Add the octopus to the sauce. Simmer for 5–10 minutes or until the octopus is tender. Pour over the pasta and serve immediately.

NOTE: *To clean octopus, use a small sharp knife and remove the gut by either cutting off the head entirely or by slicing open the head and removing the gut. Pick up the body and use your index finger to push the beak up. Remove the beak. Wash the octopus thoroughly. Cut the sac into two or three pieces.*

Use your index finger to push up from underneath the octopus so you can remove the beak.

Once the tomato sauce is cooked, add the octopus and simmer for 5–10 minutes.

Spaghetti with olive, caper and anchovy sauce

PREPARATION TIME: 15 MINUTES I TOTAL COOKING TIME: 20 MINUTES I SERVES 6

375 g (13 oz) spaghetti
4 tablespoons olive oil
2 onions, finely chopped
3 garlic cloves, finely chopped
½ teaspoon chilli flakes
6 large ripe tomatoes, diced
4 tablespoons capers in brine, rinsed and
    drained
7–8 anchovies in oil, drained, minced
150 g (5½ oz) kalamata olives
3 tablespoons chopped flat-leaf (Italian)
    parsley

1 Cook the pasta in a large saucepan of rapidly boiling salted water until *al dente*. Drain well and return to the pan to keep warm.

2 Meanwhile, heat the oil in a saucepan, add the onion and cook over medium heat for 5 minutes. Add the garlic and chilli flakes, and cook for 30 seconds, then add the tomato, capers and anchovies. Simmer over low heat for 5–10 minutes, or until thick and pulpy, then stir in the olives and parsley.

3 Stir the sauce through the pasta. Season and serve immediately with crusty bread.

NUTRITION PER SERVE
Protein 10 g; Fat 15 g; Carbohydrate 49 g; Dietary
Fibre 6.5 g; Cholesterol 2 mg; 1563 kJ (373 Cal)

The easiest way to mince the anchovies is with a mortar and pestle.

Cook the spaghetti in a saucepan of lightly salted boiling water.

Simmer the tomato and caper mixture over low heat until thick and pulpy.

Spaghetti with chilli squid

PREPARATION TIME: 10 MINUTES I TOTAL COOKING TIME: 20 MINUTES I SERVES 4

500 g (1 lb 2 oz) squid, cleaned
500 g (1 lb 2 oz) spaghetti
2 tablespoons olive oil
1 leek, chopped
2 garlic cloves, crushed
1–2 teaspoons chopped chilli
½ teaspoon cayenne pepper
425 g (15 oz) tinned chopped tomatoes
125 ml (4 fl oz/½ cup) fish stock (see NOTE)
1 tablespoon chopped basil
2 teaspoons chopped sage
1 teaspoon chopped marjoram

1 Pull the tentacles from the squid bodies. Use your fingers to pull the quills away from the pouches. Pull the skin away from the flesh and discard. Using a sharp knife, slit the tubes up one side, lay out flat and score the inside in a diamond pattern. Cut each piece into four.

2 Cook the pasta in a large saucepan of rapidly boiling salted water until *al dente*. Drain well and return to the pan to keep warm. Meanwhile, heat the oil in a large frying pan. Add the leek and cook for 2 minutes. Add the garlic and stir over low heat for 1 minute. Stir in the chilli and cayenne pepper. Add the tomato, stock and herbs. Bring to the boil. Reduce the heat and simmer for 5 minutes.

3 Add the squid to the sauce and simmer for another 5–10 minutes or until tender. Serve over the spaghetti.

NOTE: *Make fish stock by putting fish bones and trimmings, 1 chopped onion, 1 celery stalk and 1 carrot in a large saucepan, and covering with cold water. Bring to the boil, then reduce the heat and simmer for 30 minutes. Drain well, discarding the solids, and use immediately.*

NUTRITION PER SERVE
Protein 36 g; Fat 13 g; Carbohydrate 92 g; Dietary Fibre 9 g; Cholesterol 250 mg; 2671 kJ (638 Cal)

Pull the tentacles from the squid body, then pull the quill from the pouch.

Add the squid to the sauce and simmer until it is tender.

Seafood lasagne

PREPARATION TIME: 15 MINUTES | TOTAL COOKING TIME: 15 MINUTES | SERVES 4

1 tablespoon olive oil

2 garlic cloves, crushed

¼ teaspoon saffron threads

600 g (1 lb 5 oz) bottled tomato pasta sauce

750 g (1 lb 10 oz) mixed raw seafood, cut into bite-sized pieces (use scallops and peeled prawns or prepared marinara mix)

4 fresh lasagne sheets, cut into twelve 10 x 16 cm (4 x 6¼ inch) rectangles

120 g (4¼ oz) English spinach

185 g (6½ oz) mascarpone cheese

90 g (3¼ oz) grated parmesan cheese

NUTRITION PER SERVE
Protein 53 g; Fat 29 g; Carbohydrate 47 g; Dietary Fibre 5 g; Cholesterol 364 mg; 2750 kJ (655 Cal)

1 Heat the oil in a large saucepan, add the garlic, saffron and pasta sauce, reduce the heat and simmer for 8 minutes, or until thickened slightly. Add the seafood and cook for 2 minutes, or until cooked, then season. Remove from the heat.

2 Cook the pasta in a large saucepan of boiling salted water for 1–2 minutes, or until *al dente*. Remove and arrange the sheets on a tray to prevent them sticking. Blanch the spinach in the same saucepan of boiling water for 30 seconds. Remove with tongs, transfer to a colander and drain well.

3 To assemble, lay a pasta rectangle on each of four ovenproof serving plates. Spread half the mascarpone over the pasta sheets. Top with half the spinach and half the seafood sauce. Sprinkle with one-third of the parmesan. Repeat to give two layers, finishing with a third pasta sheet. Sprinkle with the remaining cheese. Place under a medium grill (broiler) for 2 minutes, or until the cheese is slightly melted. Serve immediately.

Simmer the garlic, saffron and pasta sauce until thickened slightly.

You can use the same water in which you cooked the pasta for blanching the spinach.

Lay a pasta rectangle on a plate, spread with mascarpone, then spinach and the sauce.

Pappardelle with fresh salmon and gremolata

PREPARATION TIME: 15 MINUTES | TOTAL COOKING TIME: 15 MINUTES | SERVES 4

2 large handfuls chopped flat-leaf (Italian) parsley
3 teaspoons grated lemon zest
2 garlic cloves, finely chopped
400 g (14 oz) pappardelle
3 tablespoons virgin olive oil
500 g (1 lb 2 oz) salmon fillet
2 teaspoons olive oil, extra

1 To make the gremolata, put the parsley, lemon zest and garlic in a bowl and mix together well. Cook the pasta in a large saucepan of rapidly boiling salted water until *al dente*. Drain well, transfer to a bowl, then add the virgin olive oil and toss gently. Add the gremolata and toss again.

2 Remove the skin and any bones from the salmon. Heat the extra olive oil in a frying pan and cook the salmon over medium heat for 3–4 minutes, turning once during cooking. Take care not to overcook the fish. Flake the salmon into large pieces and toss gently through the pasta. Season to taste with salt and freshly ground black pepper, divide among four warm serving plates and serve.

Make the gremolata by mixing together the parsley, lemon zest and garlic.

Remove the skin and any bones from the salmon— lift out small bones with tweezers.

NUTRITION PER SERVE
Protein 38 g; Fat 25 g; Carbohydrate 71 g; Dietary Fibre 4 g; Cholesterol 83 mg; 2755 kJ (660 Cal)

Spaghetti with smoked tuna and olives

PREPARATION TIME: 15 MINUTES | TOTAL COOKING TIME: 20 MINUTES | SERVES 4

800 g (1 lb 12 oz) vine-ripened tomatoes
375 g (13 oz) spaghetti
375 g (13 oz) tinned smoked tuna slices in oil
1 red onion, chopped
2 garlic cloves, crushed
1 teaspoon sugar
150 g (5½ oz) black olives
2 tablespoons chopped basil
75 g (2½ oz/½ cup) crumbled feta cheese

1 Score a cross in the base of each tomato.
Place the tomatoes in a bowl of boiling water for
1 minute, then plunge into cold water and peel
the skin away from the cross. Cut in half and
remove the seeds with a teaspoon. Roughly chop
the flesh. Cook the pasta in a large saucepan of
rapidly boiling salted water until *al dente*. Drain
well and return to the pan to keep warm.

2 Drain the oil from the tuna slices, reserving
1 tablespoon. Heat the reserved oil in a large
saucepan, add the onion and cook over low heat
for 3–4 minutes, or until soft but not brown.
Add the crushed garlic and cook for another
minute, then add the chopped tomatoes and
sugar. Cook over medium heat for 8–10 minutes,
or until pulpy.

3 Add the tuna slices, olives and basil, stir
well and cook for 2 minutes, or until warmed
through. Toss through the spaghetti and season
with salt and freshly ground black pepper.
Sprinkle with crumbled feta and serve.

Add the chopped tomatoes and sugar to the sauce and stir until pulpy.

Add the tuna, olives and basil to the sauce, then toss gently with the spaghetti.

NUTRITION PER SERVE
Protein 40 g; Fat 19 g; Carbohydrate 83 g; Dietary
Fibre 8 g; Cholesterol 51 mg; 2795 kJ (670 Cal)

Warm pasta and smoked salmon stack

PREPARATION TIME: 15 MINUTES | TOTAL COOKING TIME: 15 MINUTES | SERVES 4

1.5 kg (3 lb 5 oz) vine-ripened tomatoes

2 garlic cloves, crushed

1 teaspoon sugar

4 tablespoons olive oil

3 tablespoons chopped flat-leaf (Italian) parsley

6 fresh lasagne sheets

400 g (14 oz) smoked salmon

100 g (3½ oz) baby rocket (arugula) leaves

extra virgin olive oil, for drizzling

NUTRITION PER SERVE
Protein 32 g; Fat 25 g; Carbohydrate 35 g; Dietary Fibre 6.5 g; Cholesterol 48 mg; 2065 kJ (495 Cal)

1   Score a cross in the base of each tomato and place in a bowl of boiling water for 1 minute. Plunge into cold water and peel the skin away from the cross. Remove the core, then transfer to a food processor or blender and, using the pulse button, process until roughly chopped. Transfer to a saucepan with the garlic and sugar, bring to the boil, then reduce the heat and simmer for 5 minutes, or until reduced slightly. Remove from the heat and gradually whisk in the oil. Stir in the parsley and season. Keep warm.

2   Cut the lasagne sheets in half widthways to give 12 pieces, each about 12 cm (4½ inch) squares. Cook the pasta in a large saucepan of rapidly boiling water in two batches until *al dente*. Remove from the water and lay out flat to prevent sticking.

3   Place a pasta sheet on each of four plates. Set aside 4 tablespoons of the tomato mix. Spoon half the remaining tomato mixture over the pasta sheets, then half the smoked salmon and rocket leaves. Repeat to give two layers. Finish with a third sheet of pasta.

4   Top each pasta stack with a tablespoon of the tomato sauce, drizzle with a little extra virgin olive oil and serve immediately.

Peel the tomatoes and then cook to a sauce with the garlic and sugar. Add the oil and parsley.

Top the pasta with tomato sauce, then smoked salmon and rocket leaves.

Angel hair pasta with creamy garlic prawns

PREPARATION TIME: 15 MINUTES I TOTAL COOKING TIME: 15 MINUTES I SERVES 4

2 tablespoons olive oil
16 raw prawns (shrimp), peeled and deveined
1 leek, chopped
6 garlic cloves, crushed
½ teaspoon dried chilli flakes
125 ml (4 fl oz/½ cup) dry white wine
200 ml (7 fl oz) pouring (whipping) cream
250 g (9 oz) angel hair pasta
3 tablespoons chopped flat-leaf (Italian)
   parsley

1   Heat 1 tablespoon of the oil in a frying pan, season the prawns with salt and pepper, add to the pan and cook over high heat for 2–3 minutes, or until cooked through. Remove from the pan, cover and keep warm.

2   Heat the remaining oil in the same pan, add the leek and cook, stirring, over medium heat for 2–3 minutes, or until softened. Add the garlic and chilli flakes and stir for 1 minute. Pour in the wine, reduce the heat and simmer for 4 minutes, or until reduced. Add the cream and simmer for 3 minutes, or until just thickened.

3   Meanwhile, cook the pasta in a large saucepan of rapidly boiling salted water until *al dente*. Drain well and return to the pan to keep warm. Stir the parsley into the sauce and season well. Add the sauce to the pasta and stir to coat. Divide the pasta among bowls and top with the prawns.

Season the prawns with salt and pepper, then cook over high heat.

Add the cream to the sauce and stir over the heat until just thickened.

NUTRITION PER SERVE
Protein 20 g; Fat 32 g; Carbohydrate 50 g; Dietary Fibre 4.5 g; Cholesterol 143 mg; 2420 kJ (580 Cal)

Spaghetti niçoise

PREPARATION TIME: 10 MINUTES | TOTAL COOKING TIME: 15 MINUTES | SERVES 4–6

350 g (12 oz) spaghetti

8 quail eggs (or 4 hen eggs)

1 lemon

550 g (1 lb 4 oz) tinned tuna in oil

60 g (2¼ oz) pitted and halved kalamata olives

100 g (3½ oz) semi-dried (sun-blushed) tomatoes, halved lengthways

4 anchovy fillets, chopped into small pieces

3 tablespoons baby capers, drained and rinsed

3 tablespoons chopped flat-leaf (Italian) parsley

1   Cook the pasta in a large saucepan of rapidly boiling salted water until *al dente*. Drain well and return to the pan to keep warm. Meanwhile, place the eggs in a saucepan of cold water, bring to the boil and cook for 4 minutes (10 minutes for hen eggs). Drain, cool under cold water, then peel. Cut the eggs in half (or the hen eggs into quarters). Finely grate the zest of the lemon to give 1 teaspoon of grated zest. Then, squeeze the lemon to give 2 tablespoons juice.

2   Empty the tuna and its oil into a large bowl. Add the olives, tomato halves, anchovy, lemon zest and juice, capers and 2 tablespoons of the parsley. Toss the pasta gently through the tuna mixture. Garnish with the egg and the remaining parsley to serve.

Grate the lemon zest on the finest side of the grater, avoiding the white pith beneath the zest.

Toss together the pasta and tuna mixture, then garnish with the egg and parsley.

NUTRITION PER SERVE (6)
Protein 32 g; Fat 26 g; Carbohydrate 47 g; Dietary Fibre 5 g; Cholesterol 153 mg; 2300 kJ (550 Cal)

Pasta with anchovies, broccoli and basil

PREPARATION TIME: 15 MINUTES I TOTAL COOKING TIME: 25 MINUTES I SERVES 4–6

600 g (1 lb 5 oz) broccoli, cut into florets
500 g (1 lb 2 oz) orecchiette
1 tablespoon olive oil
4 garlic cloves, finely chopped
8 anchovy fillets, roughly chopped
250 ml (9 fl oz/1 cup) pouring (whipping) cream
2 large handfuls basil, torn
2 teaspoons finely grated lemon zest
100 g (3½ oz/1 cup) parmesan cheese, grated

1   Blanch the broccoli in a large saucepan of boiling salted water for 3–4 minutes. Remove and plunge into chilled water. Drain well with a slotted spoon. Cook the pasta in a large saucepan of rapidly boiling salted water until *al dente*. Drain well and return to the pan to keep warm, reserving 2 tablespoons of the cooking water.

2   Meanwhile, heat the oil in a frying pan over medium heat. Add the garlic and anchovy and cook for 1–2 minutes, or until the garlic begins to turn golden. Add the broccoli and cook for a further 5 minutes. Add the cream and half the basil and cook for 10 minutes, or until the cream has reduced and slightly thickened and the broccoli is very tender.

3   Purée half the mixture in a food processor until nearly smooth, then return to the pan with the lemon zest, half the parmesan and the reserved cooking water. Stir together well, then season. Add the warm pasta and remaining basil, and toss until well combined. Sprinkle with the remaining parmesan and serve immediately.

NUTRITION PER SERVE (6)
Protein 23 g; Fat 28 g; Carbohydrate 61 g; Dietary Fibre 9 g; Cholesterol 77 mg; 2455 kJ (585 Cal)

Blanch the broccoli in boiling salted water, then plunge into chilled water and drain well.

Add the cream and half the basil and cook until the sauce has reduced.

Purée half the mixture and then return to the pan with the lemon zest, parmesan and water.

Pasta with clams

PREPARATION TIME: 25 MINUTES + OVERNIGHT SOAKING | TOTAL COOKING TIME: 20 MINUTES | SERVES 4

2 tablespoons salt
2 tablespoons plain (all-purpose) flour
1 kg (2 lb 4 oz) clams (vongole) or pipis
500 g (1 lb 2 oz) shell pasta
1 tablespoon olive oil
2 garlic cloves, crushed
850 g (1 lb 14 oz) tinned chopped tomatoes
3 tablespoons dry red wine
2 tablespoons chopped parsley
1 teaspoon sugar

1 Blend the salt and plain flour with enough water to make a paste. Add to a large saucepan of cold water and soak the shellfish overnight. This will draw out sand from inside the shells. Scrub the shells well. Drain and rinse.

2 Cook the pasta in a large saucepan of rapidly boiling salted water until *al dente*. Drain well and return to the pan to keep warm. Meanwhile, heat the oil in a large saucepan. Add the garlic and cook over low heat for 30 seconds. Add the tomato, wine, parsley and sugar and season. Stir and bring to the boil. Reduce the heat and simmer, stirring occasionally, for 5 minutes.

3 Add the clams to the sauce and cook for 3–5 minutes, stirring occasionally, until opened. Discard any clams that do not open in the cooking time. Serve over the pasta.

Add the tomato, wine, parsley and sugar and stir well.

Add the scrubbed clams or pipis to the sauce and cook until they open.

NUTRITION PER SERVE
Protein 35 g; Fat 25 g; Carbohydrate 55 g; Dietary Fibre 7 g; Cholesterol 355 mg; 2420 kJ (580 Cal)

Cajun scallops with pasta and buttery corn sauce

PREPARATION TIME: 15 MINUTES | TOTAL COOKING TIME: 15 MINUTES | SERVES 4

350 g (12 oz) small pasta shells
20 large scallops, without roe
2 tablespoons Cajun spice mix
2 tablespoons corn oil
250 g (9 oz/1 cup) salted butter
3 garlic cloves, crushed
400 g (14 oz) tinned corn kernels, drained
3 tablespoons lime juice
4 tablespoons finely chopped coriander
    (cilantro) leaves

1 Cook the pasta in a large saucepan of rapidly boiling salted water until *al dente.* Drain well and return to the pan to keep warm. Meanwhile, pat the scallops dry with paper towel and lightly coat in the spice mix. Heat the oil in a large frying pan and cook the scallops for 1 minute on each side over high heat (ensuring they are well spaced in the pan), then remove from the pan, cover and keep warm.

2 Reduce the heat to medium, add the butter and cook for 4 minutes, or until foaming and golden brown. Remove from the heat, add the garlic, corn and lime juice. Gently toss the corn mixture through the pasta with 2 tablespoons of the coriander and season well. Divide among four serving plates, top with the scallops, drizzle with any juices and sprinkle with the remaining coriander.

NOTES: *Scallops should not be crowded when they are cooked or they will release all their juices, causing them to stew and toughen.*

To really achieve the most delicious flavours, don't use a non-stick frying pan—they can prevent the butter from properly browning and the juices from caramelising.

Cook the scallops over high heat, making sure they are well spaced in the pan.

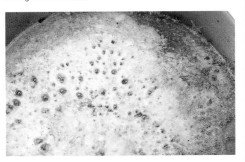

Cook the butter for 4 minutes, or until it is foaming and golden brown.

NUTRITION PER SERVE
Protein 20 g; Fat 61 g; Carbohydrate 75 g; Dietary Fibre 7 g; Cholesterol 174.5 mg; 3850 kJ (920 Cal)

Tagliatelle with salmon and creamy dill dressing

PREPARATION TIME: 10 MINUTES | TOTAL COOKING TIME: 15 MINUTES | SERVES 4

350 g (12 oz) fresh tagliatelle

3 tablespoons olive oil

3 x 200 g (7 oz) salmon fillets, skinned and boned (ask your fishmonger to do this)

3 garlic cloves, crushed

375 ml (13 fl oz/1½ cups) pouring (whipping) cream

1½ tablespoons chopped dill

1 teaspoon mustard powder

1 tablespoon lemon juice

30 g (1 oz) parmesan cheese, shaved

NUTRITION PER SERVE
Protein 45 g; Fat 66 g; Carbohydrate 51 g; Dietary Fibre 1.5 g; Cholesterol 215 mg; 4100 kJ (980 Cal)

1 Cook the pasta in a large saucepan of rapidly boiling salted water until *al dente*. Drain well, toss with 1 tablespoon of the oil and return to the pan to keep warm. Meanwhile, heat the remaining oil in a large deep frying pan and cook the salmon for 2 minutes on each side, or until crisp on the outside but still pink on the inside. Remove from the pan, cut into small cubes and keep warm.

2 In the same pan, cook the garlic for 30 seconds, or until fragrant. Add the cream, dill and mustard powder, bring to the boil, then reduce the heat and simmer, stirring, for 4–5 minutes, or until thickened. Season.

3 Add the salmon and any juices plus the lemon juice to the creamy dill sauce and stir until warmed through. Gently toss the sauce and salmon through the pasta and divide among four serving bowls. Sprinkle with the parmesan (if desired) and serve.

Cook the salmon for 2 minutes on each side to sear it, then cut into cubes.

Add the cream, dill and mustard powder and simmer until the sauce thickens.

Add the salmon and any juices to the sauce, with the lemon juice.

Fettuccine with balsamic-seared tuna

PREPARATION TIME: 15 MINUTES + 10 MINUTES MARINATING I TOTAL COOKING TIME: 15 MINUTES I SERVES 4–6

4 x 200 g (7 oz) tuna steaks

170 ml (5½ fl oz/⅔ cup) balsamic vinegar

125 ml (4 fl oz/½ cup) olive oil

1 lemon

1 garlic clove, finely chopped

1 red onion, finely chopped

2 tablespoons capers, drained and rinsed

1 large handful flat-leaf (Italian) parsley, finely chopped

500 g (1 lb 2 oz) fresh fettuccine

1   Place the tuna steaks in a non-metallic dish and cover with the balsamic vinegar. Turn to coat evenly and marinate for 10 minutes. Heat 2 tablespoons of the oil in a large frying pan over medium heat and cook the tuna for 2–3 minutes on each side. Remove from the pan, cut into small cubes and transfer to a bowl.

2   Finely grate the zest from the lemon to give ½ teaspoon zest, then squeeze the lemon to give 3 tablespoons juice. Wipe the frying pan clean, and heat 2 tablespoons of the olive oil over medium heat, then add the garlic and cook for 30 seconds. Stir in the onion and cook for 2 minutes. Add the lemon zest and capers and cook for 1 minute, then stir in the parsley and cook for 1 minute. Add the lemon juice and remaining oil and gently toss together. Season to taste.

3   Meanwhile, cook the pasta in a large saucepan of rapidly boiling salted water until *al dente*. Drain well, return to the pan and toss with the caper mixture. Divide the pasta among serving bowls and arrange the tuna pieces over the top.

Sear the tuna over medium heat and then cut it into bite-sized cubes.

Cook the garlic, onion, lemon zest, capers and parsley, then add the lemon juice.

NUTRITION PER SERVE (6)
Fat 26 g; Protein 43 g; Carbohydrate 60 g; Dietary Fibre 4.5 g; Cholesterol 48 mg; 2740 kJ (655 Cal)

Tagliatelle with salmon roe and herb breadcrumbs

PREPARATION TIME: 15 MINUTES I TOTAL COOKING TIME: 20 MINUTES I SERVES 6

8 slices white bread
250 g (9 oz) mascarpone cheese
2 egg yolks
4 garlic cloves, peeled
200 ml (7 fl oz) olive oil
500 g (1 lb 2 oz) fresh tagliatelle
3 tablespoons chopped dill
100 g (3½ oz/1 cup) grated parmesan cheese
60 g (2¼ oz) salmon roe

1 Place the slices of bread in a food processor or blender and process until fine breadcrumbs form. Remove from the food processor. Place the mascarpone, egg yolks and 1 garlic clove in the food processor or blender and process until smooth. With the motor running, gradually add half the oil in a thin stream.

2 Cook the pasta in a large pan of rapidly boiling salted water until *al dente*. Drain well and return to the pan to keep warm. Meanwhile, heat the remaining oil in a heavy-based frying pan and cook the remaining garlic over medium heat for 2–3 minutes, or until golden brown. Remove the cloves from the oil and discard. Add the fresh breadcrumbs to the warm oil and cook over low heat for 15 minutes, or until golden and crunchy. Remove from the pan and drain on paper towels. When cool, stir in the dill and season lightly with salt and freshly ground black pepper.

3 Add the mascarpone mixture and the parmesan to the pasta and toss together well. Divide among six serving plates, sprinkle with the breadcrumbs, top with the salmon roe and serve immediately.

Process the mascarpone, egg yolks and garlic until smooth.

Flavour the oil with garlic and then use to cook the breadcrumbs until brown and crunchy.

NUTRITION PER SERVE
Protein 26 g; Fat 54 g; Carbohydrate 78 g; Dietary Fibre 6 g; Cholesterol 152 mg; 3745 kJ (895 Cal)

Vegetarian pasta

Blue cheese gnocchi

PREPARATION TIME: 20 MINUTES | TOTAL COOKING TIME: 20 MINUTES | SERVES 4

500 g (1 lb 2 oz) all-purpose potatoes,
  quartered
155 g (5½ oz/1¼ cups) plain (all-purpose)
  flour

SAUCE
300 ml (10½ fl oz) pouring (whipping) cream
125 g (4½ oz) gorgonzola cheese, roughly
  chopped
2 tablespoons snipped chives

1 Cook the potatoes in boiling salted water for 15–20 minutes or in the microwave until tender. Stir through a generous amount of salt. Drain the potatoes then mash until completely smooth. Transfer to a bowl.

2 Sprinkle the flour into the bowl with one hand while kneading it into the potato mixture with the other hand. Continue kneading until all the flour is worked in and the dough is smooth. This should take a few minutes and will be sticky at first.

3 Divide the dough into three and roll each portion into a sausage that is 2 cm (¾ inch) thick. Cut into 2.5 cm (1 inch) lengths and, using floured hands, press each gnocchi against a fork to flatten it and indent one side (the indentation helps the sauce to stick to the cooked gnocchi).

4 Bring a large saucepan of water to the boil. When rapidly boiling, drop in the gnocchi, then reduce the heat and simmer until the gnocchi rise to the surface. This will take 2–3 minutes. Lift the gnocchi out of the water with a slotted spoon and drain well. Keep warm on a serving dish.

5 Put the cream in a small saucepan and bring to the boil. Boil rapidly, stirring constantly, for about 5 minutes, or until the sauce has reduced by a third. Remove from the heat and stir through the cheese. Season and pour over the gnocchi. Scatter the chives over the top and serve immediately.

NUTRITION PER SERVE
Protein 20 g; Fat 45 g; Carbohydrate 45 g; Dietary Fibre 3.5 g; Cholesterol 130 mg; 2736 kJ (655 Cal)

Add the flour with one hand while kneading it into the potato with the other.

Gently knead the mixture until all the flour is mixed in and the dough is smooth.

Press each gnocchi against a fork to flatten it and indent one side.

Fettuccine with zucchini

PREPARATION TIME: 15 MINUTES | TOTAL COOKING TIME: 15 MINUTES | SERVES 4–6

500 g (1 lb 2 oz) tagliatelle or fettuccine
60 g (2¼ oz/¼ cup) salted butter
2 garlic cloves, crushed
500 g (1 lb 2 oz) zucchini (courgettes), grated
75 g (2½ oz/¾ cup) grated parmesan cheese
250 ml (9 fl oz/1 cup) olive oil
16 basil leaves

1   Cook the pasta in a large saucepan of rapidly boiling salted water until *al dente*. Drain well and return to the pan to keep warm.

2   Meanwhile, heat the butter in a deep heavy-based saucepan over low heat until it is foaming. Add the garlic and cook for 1 minute. Add the zucchini and cook, stirring occasionally, for 1–2 minutes or until the zucchini has softened.

3   Add the sauce to the pasta. Add the parmesan cheese and toss well.

4   To make basil leaves crisp, heat the oil in a small frying pan, add two leaves at a time and cook for 1 minute or until crisp. Drain on paper towels. Serve with the pasta.

NUTRITION PER SERVE (6)
Protein 15 g; Fat 53 g; Carbohydrate 60 g; Dietary Fibre 5.5 g; Cholesterol 37 mg; 3245 kJ (775 Cal)

Coarsely grate the zucchini and then fry with the garlic until softened.

Toss the zucchini into the pasta and then add the grated parmesan.

Fry the basil leaves in a little oil until they are crisp; then drain on paper towels.

Bucatini with eggplant and mushrooms

PREPARATION TIME: 20 MINUTES | TOTAL COOKING TIME: 25 MINUTES | SERVES 4–6

2 tablespoons olive oil
250 g (9 oz) mushrooms, sliced
1 eggplant (aubergine), diced
2 garlic cloves, crushed
820 g (1 lb 13 oz) tinned chopped tomatoes
500 g (1 lb 2 oz) bucatini or spaghetti
1 large handful chopped parsley (optional)

1 Heat the oil in a pan and cook the mushrooms, eggplant and garlic, stirring, for 4 minutes. Add the tomato, cover and simmer for 15 minutes.

2 Meanwhile, cook the pasta in a large saucepan of rapidly boiling salted water until *al dente*. Drain well and return to the pan to keep warm. Season the sauce with salt and freshly ground black pepper and stir in the parsley. Toss with the pasta and serve immediately.

HINT: If the pasta is cooked before you are ready to serve you can prevent it sticking together by tossing it with a little olive oil after draining.

NUTRITION PER SERVE (6)
Protein 12 g; Fat 8 g; Carbohydrate 65 g; Dietary Fibre 8 g; Cholesterol 0 mg; 1600 kJ (383 Cal)

Wipe the mushrooms clean and slice them. Cut the eggplant into small cubes.

Heat the oil in a saucepan and cook the mushrooms, eggplant and garlic.

Add the chopped parsley to the sauce just before tossing with the pasta.

Fresh vegetable lasagne with rocket

PREPARATION TIME: 20 MINUTES | TOTAL COOKING TIME: 20 MINUTES | SERVES 4

BALSAMIC SYRUP
4 tablespoons balsamic vinegar
1½ tablespoons brown sugar

155 g (5½ oz/1 cup) fresh or frozen peas
16 asparagus spears, trimmed and cut into
    short lengths
2 large zucchini (courgettes), cut into thin
    ribbons
2 fresh lasagne sheets (each sheet 24 x
    35 cm/9½ x 14 inches)
100 g (3½ oz) rocket (arugula) leaves
1 very large handful basil, torn
2 tablespoons extra virgin olive oil
250 g (9 oz/1 cup) low-fat ricotta cheese
150 g (5½ oz) semi-dried (sun-blushed)
    tomatoes
parmesan cheese shaved, to serve

1   To make the syrup, place the vinegar and brown sugar in a small saucepan and stir over medium heat until the sugar dissolves. Reduce the heat and simmer for 3–4 minutes, or until the sauce becomes syrupy. Remove from the heat.

2   Bring a large saucepan of salted water to the boil. Blanch the peas, asparagus and zucchini in separate batches until just tender, removing each batch with a slotted spoon and refreshing in cold water. Reserve the cooking liquid and return to the boil.

3   Cook the lasagne sheets in the boiling water for 1–2 minutes, or until *al dente*. Refresh in cold water and drain well. Cut each sheet in half lengthways.

4   Toss the vegetables and the rocket with the basil and olive oil. Season.

5   To assemble, place one strip of pasta on a serving plate—one-third on the centre of the plate and two-thirds overhanging one side. Place a small amount of the salad on the centre one-third, topped with some ricotta and tomato. Season lightly and fold over one-third of the lasagne sheet. Top with another layer of salad, ricotta and tomato. Fold back the final layer of pasta and garnish with a little salad and tomato. Repeat with the remaining pasta strips, salad, ricotta and tomato to make four individual servings. Just before serving, drizzle with the balsamic syrup and sprinkle with parmesan shavings.

NUTRITION PER SERVE
Protein 18 g; Fat 16 g; Carbohydrate 36 g; Dietary Fibre 6 g; Cholesterol 63 mg; 1515 kJ (360 Cal)

Simmer the balsamic vinegar and brown sugar until the liquid becomes syrupy.

Toss the peas, asparagus, zucchini, rocket, basil and olive oil together.

Fold one-third of the lasagne sheet over the salad mix, ricotta and tomato.

Pasta with ricotta, chilli and herbs

PREPARATION TIME: 15 MINUTES I TOTAL COOKING TIME: 20 MINUTES I SERVES 4

500 g (1 lb 2 oz) spiral pasta or penne
3 tablespoons olive oil
3 garlic cloves, crushed
2 teaspoons very finely chopped chilli
2 large handfuls flat-leaf (Italian) parsley
   leaves, roughly chopped
1 handful basil leaves, shredded
2 very large handfuls oregano leaves, roughly
   chopped
200 g (7 oz) ricotta cheese, cut into small
   cubes

1   Cook the pasta in a large saucepan of rapidly boiling salted water until *al dente*. Drain well and return to the pan to keep warm. Meanwhile, heat the oil in a non-stick heavy-based frying pan. Add the garlic and chilli to the frying pan and stir for 1 minute over low heat.

2   Pour the contents of the frying pan over the pasta and add the parsley, basil and oregano. Season to taste and toss well.

3   Add the cubes of ricotta to the pasta and serve immediately.

NUTRITION PER SERVE
Protein 20 g; Fat 20 g; Carbohydrate 90 g; Dietary Fibre 7 g; Cholesterol 24 mg; 2635 kJ (630 Cal)

Heat the oil in a frying pan and cook the garlic and chilli for 1 minute over low heat.

Pour the contents of the frying pan over the pasta, add the herbs and season.

Cut the ricotta into small cubes and add to the pasta salad.

Pasta with baby spinach, pumpkin and tomato

PREPARATION TIME: 15 MINUTES | TOTAL COOKING TIME: 1 HOUR | SERVES 4

750 g (1 lb 10 oz) pumpkin (winter squash)
2 tablespoons olive oil (see NOTES)
16 garlic cloves, unpeeled
250 g (9 oz) cherry tomatoes, halved
500 g (1 lb 2 oz) pasta
200 g (7 oz) baby English spinach leaves
200 g (7 oz) marinated Persian feta cheese
    (see NOTES)
3 tablespoons sherry vinegar
2 tablespoons walnut oil

1 Preheat the oven to 200°C (400°F/Gas 6). Cut the pumpkin into large cubes, place in a roasting tin and drizzle with oil. Roast for 30 minutes, then add the garlic. Arrange the tomatoes on a baking tray. Put all the vegetables in the oven and roast for 10–15 minutes, or until tender. Don't overcook the tomatoes or they will break up.

2 Cook the pasta in a large saucepan of rapidly boiling salted water until *al dente*. Drain well and return to the pan to keep warm.

3 Toss together the pasta, tomatoes, pumpkin, garlic and spinach.

4 Drain the feta, reserving 3 tablespoons marinade. Whisk this with the sherry vinegar and walnut oil. Pour over the pasta and sprinkle with feta.

NOTES: *If you can find it, use parmesan-infused olive oil. It is available at gourmet food stores and adds depth of flavour.*

Persian feta is softer and creamier than other feta and is marinated in oil, herbs and garlic.

VARIATION: *Toss in 200 g (7 oz) marinated kalamata olives for added flavour.*

NUTRITION PER SERVE
Protein 29 g; Fat 34 g; Carbohydrate 105 g; Dietary Fibre 13 g; Cholesterol 34 mg; 3524 kJ (842 Cal)

Drizzle the cubes of pumpkin with olive oil, using parmesan-infused oil if available.

Roast the pumpkin, garlic and tomatoes until they are tender.

Potato gnocchi with tomato and basil sauce

PREPARATION TIME: 1 HOUR | TOTAL COOKING TIME: 50 MINUTES | SERVES 4–6

TOMATO SAUCE
1 tablespoon oil
1 onion, chopped
1 celery stalk, chopped
2 carrots, chopped
850 g (1 lb 14 oz) tinned chopped tomatoes
1 teaspoon sugar
1 very large handful basil, chopped

1 kg (2 lb 4 oz) all-purpose potatoes, roughly
    chopped
30 g (1 oz) salted butter
250 g (9 oz/2 cups) plain (all-purpose) flour
2 eggs, beaten
grated parmesan cheese, for serving

NUTRITION PER SERVE (6)
Protein 15 g; Fat 10 g; Carbohydrate 60 g; Dietary
Fibre 5 g; Cholesterol 75 mg; 1680 kJ (400 Cal)

1 To make the tomato sauce, heat the oil in a large frying pan and cook the onion, celery and carrots for 5 minutes, stirring regularly. Add the tomato and sugar and season. Bring to the boil, reduce the heat to very low and simmer for 20 minutes. Mix until smooth in a food processor. Add the basil leaves and set aside.

2 To make the gnocchi, cook the potatoes in boiling water for 15 minutes or until very tender. Drain well and mash until smooth. Using a wooden spoon, stir in the butter and the flour, then mix in the eggs. Leave to cool.

3 Turn the potato mixture out onto a floured surface and divide in two. Roll each half into a long sausage shape. Cut into 3–4 cm (1¼–1½ inch) pieces and press each piece with the back of a fork to give the gnocchi ridges.

4 Bring a large saucepan of salted water to the boil, add the gnocchi and cook for 3 minutes, or until they rise to the surface. Drain with a slotted spoon and serve with the tomato sauce and grated parmesan cheese.

Add the tomato, sugar and seasoning to the frying vegetables.

Use a wooden spoon to mix the eggs into the mashed potato.

Press each piece of gnocchi with the back of a fork to give the traditional ridges

Tagliatelle with asparagus and herbs

PREPARATION TIME: 15 MINUTES I TOTAL COOKING TIME: 15 MINUTES I SERVES 4–6

500 g (1 lb 2 oz) tagliatelle
175 g (6 oz) asparagus
2 tablespoons salted butter
1 tablespoon chopped parsley
1 tablespoon chopped basil
310 ml (10¾ fl oz/1¼ cups) pouring
  (whipping) cream
60 g (2¼ oz) grated parmesan cheese

1   Cook the pasta in a large saucepan of rapidly boiling salted water until *al dente*. Drain well and return to the pan to keep warm.

2   Meanwhile, snap the woody ends from the asparagus and cut the stems into short lengths. Heat the butter in a saucepan and stir the asparagus over medium heat for 2 minutes or until just tender.

3   Add the chopped parsley and basil, cream, salt and pepper and cook for 2 minutes.

4   Add the parmesan to the sauce and stir well. Toss through the pasta and serve in warmed bowls.

NOTE: *Will serve eight people as a starter.*

NUTRITION PER SERVE (6)
Protein 14 g; Fat 30 g; Carbohydrate 60 g; Dietary Fibre 4 g; Cholesterol 95mg; 2418 kJ (580 Cal)

Snap the woody ends from the asparagus and then cut the spears into short pieces.

Add the chopped parsley and basil, cream and salt and pepper.

Add the parmesan to the sauce and then toss with the warm pasta.

Linguine with red capsicum sauce

PREPARATION TIME: 20 MINUTES | TOTAL COOKING TIME: 25 MINUTES | SERVES 4–6

3 red capsicums (peppers)
3 tablespoons olive oil
1 large onion, sliced
2 garlic cloves, crushed
¼–½ teaspoon chilli flakes or powder
125 ml (4 fl oz/½ cup) pouring (whipping)
   cream
2 tablespoons chopped oregano
500 g (1 lb 2 oz) linguine or spaghetti

1 Halve each capsicum, removing the membrane and seeds and cut into large pieces. Place skin side up under a hot grill (broiler) and cook for 8 minutes or until black and blistered. Cover with a damp tea towel (dish towel) and allow to cool. Peel off the skin and cut the capsicum into thin strips.

2 Heat the oil in a large heavy-based saucepan. Add the onion and cook, stirring, over low heat for 8 minutes or until soft. Add the capsicum, garlic, chilli flakes or powder and cream and cook for 2 minutes, stirring occasionally. Season and add the oregano.

3 Meanwhile, cook the pasta in a large saucepan of rapidly boiling salted water until *al dente.* Drain well and return to the pan to keep warm. Add the sauce to the pasta and toss well before serving.

HINT: *If you use dried oregano use about one-third of the quantity as dried herbs are stronger in flavour.*

VARIATION: *For a stronger capsicum flavour, omit the cream.*

Grill the capsicum until the skin is blackened and will peel away easily.

Add the capsicum, garlic, chilli and cream, and cook for 2 minutes.

NUTRITION PER SERVE (6)
Protein 11 g; Fat 20 g; Carbohydrate 62 g; Dietary Fibre 5 g; Cholesterol 62 mg; 1970 kJ (470 Cal)

Pumpkin and ricotta lasagne with lime butter

PREPARATION TIME: 30 MINUTES | TOTAL COOKING TIME: 30 MINUTES | SERVES 4 AS A STARTER

½ butternut pumpkin (squash) (about 600 g/ 1 lb 5 oz), peeled and seeded

2 tablespoons olive oil

3 teaspoons finely chopped rosemary

1 teaspoon sea salt flakes

3 tablespoons lime juice

3 tablespoons dry white wine

3 tablespoons vegetable stock

3 French shallots (eschalots) finely chopped

1 garlic clove, crushed

¼ teaspoon white pepper

1 tablespoon pouring (whipping) cream

150 g (5½ oz) salted butter, chilled and cut into small cubes

2 teaspoons finely diced mustard fruit (see NOTE)

100 g (3½ oz) fresh lasagne sheets, cut into eight 8 cm (3¼ inch) squares

100 g (3½ oz) ricotta cheese

1 amaretti biscuit (cookie), crushed (optional)

small sprigs fresh rosemary, to garnish

1 Preheat the oven to 200°C (400°F/Gas 6). Cut the pumpkin in half, then each half into eight slices. Combine half the oil, 2 teaspoons of the rosemary and salt in a bowl and toss the slices through the mixture. Put them in a single layer on a baking tray and bake for 25–30 minutes, or until cooked and slightly caramelised. Remove from the oven, cover and keep warm.

2 Meanwhile, combine the lime juice, wine, stock, shallots, garlic, white pepper and the remaining rosemary in a small saucepan and simmer for 15–20 minutes, or until the liquid has reduced to about 2 tablespoons. Strain into a small clean saucepan, then add the cream and simmer for 2–3 minutes, or until thickened slightly. Whisk in the butter a few cubes at a time until all the butter is used and the sauce is thick and glossy. Remove from the heat and stir in the mustard fruit. Cover and set aside. Fill a large saucepan with water, add the remaining oil and bring to the boil. Reduce to a simmer. Add the lasagne in batches and cook, stirring, for 1–2 minutes, or until *al dente*. Drain well.

3 Place one lasagne square on each plate; two slices of pumpkin onto each square; top with one quarter of the ricotta; another two slices of pumpkin; finish with a layer of lasagne. Spoon a little of the lime butter around the lasagne on the plate. Sprinkle with the crushed amaretti and fresh rosemary.

NOTE: *Mustard fruit is a piquant fruit relish made from crystallised fruits preserved in white wine, honey and mustard.*

NUTRITION PER SERVE
Protein 11 g; Fat 16 g; Carbohydrate 34 g; Dietary Fibre 4.5 g; Cholesterol 20 mg; 1413 kJ (340 Cal)

Bake the pumpkin in a single layer until it is cooked through and just caramelised.

Add a few cubes of butter at a time and whisk until thick and glossy.

Spread one quarter of the ricotta over the pumpkin pieces.

Fettuccine with sweet potato, feta and olives

PREPARATION TIME: 15 MINUTES | TOTAL COOKING TIME: 35 MINUTES | SERVES 6

1.5 kg (3 lb 5 oz) orange sweet potato, cut into small cubes
4 tablespoons olive oil
4 garlic cloves, crushed
2 tablespoons salted butter
4 red onions, sliced into thin wedges
500 g (1 lb 2 oz) fresh plain or spinach fettuccine
400 g (14 oz) soft feta cheese, diced
200 g (7 oz) small black olives
2 large handfuls basil, torn

1 Preheat the oven to 200°C (400°F/Gas 6). Place the sweet potato, oil and garlic in a bowl and toss to coat the sweet potato. Lay out the sweet potato in a roasting tin and roast for 15 minutes. Turn and roast for another 15 minutes, until tender and golden—make sure the sweet potato is not too soft or it will not hold its shape. Keep warm.

2 Meanwhile, melt the butter in a deep frying pan and cook the onion over low heat, stirring occasionally, for 25–30 minutes, or until soft and slightly caramelised.

3 Cook the pasta in a large saucepan of rapidly boiling salted water until *al dente*. Drain well and return to the pan. Add the onion to the pasta and toss together. Add the sweet potato, feta, olives and basil and gently toss. Serve drizzled with extra virgin olive oil.

Cook the onion in the butter over low heat until soft and caramelised.

NUTRITION PER SERVE
Protein 28 g; Fat 33 g; Carbohydrate 91 g; Dietary Fibre 7 g; Cholesterol 124 mg; 3195 kJ (765 Cal)

Roast pumpkin sauce on pappardelle

PREPARATION TIME: 15 MINUTES | TOTAL COOKING TIME: 35 MINUTES | SERVES 4

1.5 kg (3 lb 5 oz) butternut pumpkin (squash),
   cut into small cubes
4 garlic cloves, crushed
3 teaspoons thyme leaves, plus extra, to serve
100 ml (3½ fl oz) olive oil
500 g (1 lb 2 oz) pappardelle
2 tablespoons pouring (whipping) cream
185 ml (6 fl oz/¾ cup) hot chicken stock
30 g (1 oz) shaved parmesan cheese, to serve

1   Preheat the oven to 200°C (400°F/Gas 6).
Put the pumpkin, garlic, thyme leaves and
3 tablespoons of the olive oil in a bowl and toss
together. Season with salt, transfer to a baking
tray and cook for 30 minutes, or until tender
and golden. Meanwhile, cook the pasta in a large
saucepan of rapidly boiling salted water until
al dente. Drain well and return to the pan. Toss
through the remaining oil and keep warm.

2   Place the pumpkin and cream in a food
processor or blender and process until smooth.
Add the hot stock and process until smooth.
Season with salt and freshly ground black pepper
and gently toss through the pasta. Serve with the
parmesan and extra thyme leaves.

NOTE: *The sauce becomes thick on standing, so
serve immediately.*

Toss the pumpkin through the herbs and oil, then season with salt and roast until soft.

Put the cooked pumpkin and cream in a food processor and mix until smooth.

NUTRITION PER SERVE
Protein 26 g; Fat 30 g; Carbohydrate 110 g; Dietary
Fibre 8 g; Cholesterol 43 mg; 3400 kJ (810 Cal)

Tagliatelle with sweet tomato and walnut sauce

PREPARATION TIME: 20 MINUTES | TOTAL COOKING TIME: 40 MINUTES | SERVES 4–6

4 ripe roma (plum) tomatoes
1 tablespoon olive oil
1 onion, finely chopped
1 celery stalk, finely chopped
1 carrot, grated
2 tablespoons chopped parsley
1 teaspoon red wine vinegar
3 tablespoons dry white wine
500 g (1 lb 2 oz) tagliatelle or fettuccine
1 tablespoon olive oil, extra
90 g (3¼ oz/¾ cup) walnuts, roughly
    chopped
grated parmesan cheese, for serving

1 Score a cross on the base of each tomato, place in boiling water for 1 minute, then plunge into cold water. Peel the skin away from the cross and roughly chop the tomatoes.

2 Heat the oil in a large heavy-based saucepan and cook the onion and celery for 5 minutes over low heat, stirring regularly. Add the tomato, carrot, parsley and vinegar. Reduce the heat and simmer for 25 minutes. Season to taste.

3 Meanwhile, cook the pasta in a large saucepan of rapidly boiling salted water until *al dente*. Drain well and return to the pan to keep warm.

4 Heat the extra oil in a frying pan and stir the walnuts over low heat for 5 minutes. Toss the pasta and sauce together and serve topped with walnuts and parmesan cheese.

NUTRITION PER SERVE (6)
Protein 13 g; Fat 10 g; Carbohydrate 61 g; Dietary Fibre 6 g; Cholesterol 7 mg; 1654 kJ (395 Cal)

Peel the carrot if it needs it, before grating. Peel the tomatoes and roughly chop.

Cook the onion and celery before adding the tomatoes, carrot, parsley and vinegar.

Gently fry the walnuts over low heat to bring out the flavour.

Penne with rustic lentil sauce

PREPARATION TIME: 10 MINUTES | TOTAL COOKING TIME: 30 MINUTES | SERVES 4

1 litre (35 fl oz/4 cups) vegetable or chicken stock
350 g (12 oz) penne
4 tablespoons virgin olive oil, plus extra for serving
1 onion, chopped
2 carrots, diced
3 celery stalks, diced
3 garlic cloves, crushed
1 tablespoon chopped thyme, plus 1 teaspoon, extra
400 g (14 oz) tinned lentils, drained

1 Boil the chicken stock in a large saucepan for 10 minutes, or until reduced by half. Meanwhile, cook the pasta in a large saucepan of rapidly boiling salted water until *al dente*. Drain well and toss with 2 tablespoons of the olive oil.

2 Heat the remaining oil in a large, deep frying pan, add the onion, carrot and celery and cook over medium heat for 10 minutes, or until browned. Add two-thirds of the crushed garlic and 1 tablespoon of the thyme and cook for a further 1 minute. Add the stock, bring to the boil and cook for 8 minutes, or until tender. Stir in the lentils and heat through.

3 Stir in the remaining garlic and thyme and season well—the stock should be slightly syrupy at this point. Combine the pasta with the lentil sauce in a large bowl and drizzle with virgin olive oil to serve.

Drain the pasta well and toss with a little olive oil to prevent it sticking.

Stir the remaining garlic and thyme into the sauce and season well.

NUTRITION PER SERVE
Protein 17 g; Fat 18 g; Carbohydrate 72 g; Dietary Fibre 9 g; Cholesterol 0 mg; 2165 kJ (515 Cal)

Rotelle with chickpeas, tomato and parsley

PREPARATION TIME: 10 MINUTES | TOTAL COOKING TIME: 15 MINUTES | SERVES 4

375 g (13 oz) rotelle
1 tablespoon ground cumin
125 ml (4 fl oz/½ cup) olive oil
1 red onion, halved and thinly sliced
3 garlic cloves, crushed
400 g (14 oz) tinned chickpeas, drained
3 large tomatoes, diced
1 large handful chopped flat-leaf (Italian)
    parsley
3 tablespoons lemon juice

1   Cook the pasta in a large saucepan of rapidly boiling salted water until *al dente*. Drain well and return to the pan to keep warm.

2   Meanwhile, heat a large frying pan over medium heat, add the cumin and cook, tossing, for 1 minute, or until fragrant. Remove from the pan. Heat half the oil in the same pan and cook the onion over medium heat for 2–3 minutes, or until soft. Stir in the garlic, chickpeas, tomato and parsley and stir until warmed through. Gently toss through the pasta.

3   Place the lemon juice, cumin and remaining oil in a jar with a lid and shake together well. Add the dressing to the saucepan with the pasta and chickpea mixture, return to the stovetop over low heat and stir until warmed through. Season well with salt and freshly ground black pepper. Serve hot with grated parmesan, or serve cold. If serving cold, rinse the pasta under cold water before adding the chickpea mixture and do not return to the heat.

Add the garlic, chickpeas, tomato and parsley and stir to warm through.

Mix together the lemon juice, cumin and remaining oil to make a dressing.

NUTRITION PER SERVE
Protein 17 g; Fat 27 g; Carbohydrate 80 g; Dietary Fibre 10 g; Cholesterol 0 mg; 2655 kJ (635 Cal)

Tagliatelle with asparagus, peas and herb sauce

PREPARATION TIME: 20 MINUTES | TOTAL COOKING TIME: 25 MINUTES | SERVES 4

375 g (13 oz) tagliatelle
2 leeks, thinly sliced
250 ml (9 fl oz/1 cup) chicken or vegetable
    stock
3 garlic cloves, crushed
250 g (9 oz/1½ cups) shelled fresh peas
1 tablespoon finely chopped mint
400 g (14 oz) asparagus spears, cut into
    5 cm (2 inch) lengths
15 g (½ oz) finely chopped parsley
30 g (1 oz) shredded basil
4 tablespoons pouring (whipping) cream
pinch of grated nutmeg
1 tablespoon grated parmesan cheese
2 tablespoons extra virgin olive oil, to serve

1   Cook the pasta in a large saucepan of rapidly boiling salted water until *al dente*. Drain well and return to the pan to keep warm.

2   Put the leeks and 125 ml (4 fl oz/½ cup) of the stock in a large, deep, frying pan. Cook over low heat, stirring often, for 4–5 minutes. Stir in the garlic, peas and mint and cook for 1 minute. Add the remaining stock and 125 ml (4 fl oz/ ½ cup) water and bring to the boil. Simmer for 5 minutes. Add the asparagus, parsley and basil and season well. Simmer for 3–4 minutes, or until the asparagus is just tender. Gradually increase the heat to thicken the sauce until it will just coat a spoon. Stir in the cream, nutmeg and parmesan and season.

3   Add the sauce to the tagliatelle and toss lightly to coat. Serve drizzled with the extra virgin olive oil.

NUTRITION PER SERVE
Protein 21 g; Fat 11 g; Carbohydrate 76 g; Dietary Fibre 9 g; Cholesterol 32 mg; 2080 kJ (495 Cal)

Stir the garlic, peas and mint into the stock and leek mixture.

Stir in the cream, nutmeg and grated parmesan and check the seasoning.

Cotelli with capers, bocconcini and basil oil

PREPARATION TIME: 10 MINUTES I TOTAL COOKING TIME: 20 MINUTES I SERVES 4–6

125 ml (4 fl oz/½ cup) olive oil
125 g (4½ oz) capers in brine, drained and
   rinsed
500 g (1 lb 2 oz) cotelli
2 tablespoons lemon juice
3 very large handfuls basil
35 g (1¼ oz/⅓ cup) grated parmesan cheese
250 g (9 oz) cherry tomatoes, quartered
8 bocconcini (fresh baby mozzarella cheese),
   quartered
extra virgin olive oil, for serving

1   Heat half the oil in a frying pan, add the
capers and cook over high heat for 3–4 minutes,
or until crisp and golden. Drain on paper towels
and set aside.

2   Cook the pasta in a large saucepan of rapidly
boiling salted water until *al dente*. Drain well and
return to the pan to keep warm. Meanwhile, mix
the lemon juice, 2 very large handfuls of the basil
and the remaining oil in a food processor until
smooth. Season.

3   Roughly tear the remaining basil leaves,
then toss through the warm pasta with the basil
mixture, 2 tablespoons of the parmesan and the
cherry tomatoes. Spoon into warmed bowls and
top with the bocconcini and capers. Drizzle with
the extra virgin olive oil and garnish with the
remaining grated parmesan. Serve immediately.

Cook the capers over high heat until they are crisp
and golden.

Mix the lemon juice, basil and olive oil in a food
processor until smooth.

NUTRITION PER SERVE (6)
Protein 21 g; Fat 26 g; Carbohydrate 61 g; Dietary
Fibre 5.5 g; Cholesterol 23.5 mg; 2375 kJ (565 Cal)

Linguine with broccoli, pine nuts and lemon

PREPARATION TIME: 15 MINUTES | TOTAL COOKING TIME: 15 MINUTES | SERVES 4–6

500 g (1 lb 2 oz) linguine
600 g (1 lb 5 oz) broccoli, cut into small florets
90 g (3¼ oz) pine nuts
125 ml (4 fl oz/½ cup) extra virgin olive oil
2 teaspoons finely grated lemon zest
3 tablespoons lemon juice
1 teaspoon dried chilli flakes
60 g (2¼ oz) finely grated parmesan cheese

1 Cook the pasta in a large saucepan of rapidly boiling salted water until *al dente*. Drain well and return to the pan to keep warm. Meanwhile, bring a saucepan of water to the boil and cook the broccoli for 2 minutes, or until just tender but still bright green. Drain and set aside.

2 Heat a large non-stick frying pan and dry-fry the pine nuts for 2–3 minutes, or until just golden, shaking the pan to prevent them burning. Remove from the pan and roughly chop. Reduce the heat to low, add the oil and lemon zest to the frying pan and gently heat until fragrant. Add the broccoli, chopped pine nuts, lemon juice and chilli flakes and stir until warmed through. Season with salt and pepper. Add to the pasta with the parmesan and toss to combine. Divide among serving bowls.

Cook the pasta in a large saucepan of rapidly boiling water until *al dente*.

Add the broccoli, chopped pine nuts, lemon juice and chilli flakes and warm through.

NUTRITION PER SERVE (6)
Protein 19 g; Fat 27 g; Carbohydrate 60 g; Dietary Fibre 9 g; Cholesterol 8 mg; 2355 kJ (560 Cal)

Roasted sweet potato and ditalini patties

PREPARATION TIME: 15 MINUTES | TOTAL COOKING TIME: 1 HOUR 10 MINUTES | SERVES 4

800 g (1 lb 12 oz) orange sweet potatoes
90 g (3¼ oz/½ cup) ditalini
30 g (1 oz) pine nuts, toasted
2 garlic cloves, crushed
4 tablespoons finely chopped basil
60 g (2¼ oz) grated parmesan cheese
35 g (1¼ oz/⅓ cup) dry breadcrumbs
plain (all-purpose) flour, for dusting
olive oil, for shallow-frying

1 Preheat the oven to 250°C (500°F/Gas 9). Pierce the whole sweet potatoes several times with a fork, then place in a roasting tin and roast for about 1 hour, or until soft. Remove from the oven and cool. Meanwhile, cook the pasta in a large saucepan of rapidly boiling salted water until *al dente*. Drain well and rinse under cold water.

2 Peel the sweet potato and mash with a potato masher or fork. Add the pine nuts, garlic, basil, parmesan, breadcrumbs and the pasta and mix together. Season.

3 Shape the mixture into eight even patties with floured hands, then lightly dust the patties with flour. Heat the oil in a large frying pan and cook the patties in batches over medium heat for 2 minutes on each side, or until golden and heated through. Drain on crumpled paper towels, sprinkle with salt and serve immediately.

NOTE: *If you don't have much time, drop spoonfuls of the mixture into the pan and flatten with an oiled spatula.*

SERVING SUGGESTION: *The patties are great with aïoli—mix 1 clove of crushed garlic into 90 g (3¼ oz/⅓ cup) mayonnaise with a squeeze of lemon juice and season well.*

NUTRITION PER SERVE
Protein 14 g; Fat 15 g; Carbohydrate 51 g; Dietary Fibre 6 g; Cholesterol 12 mg; 1650 kJ (395 Cal)

Roast the sweet potatoes in their skins for an hour and then pierce to check they are soft.

Peel the sweet potatoes and then mash with a potato masher or fork.

Keep your hands lightly floured when shaping the patties so they don't stick.

Farmhouse pasta

PREPARATION TIME: 10 MINUTES | TOTAL COOKING TIME: 15 MINUTES | SERVES 4

375 g (13 oz) pasta
1 large all-purpose potato, cut into small cubes
400 g (14 oz) broccoli
4 tablespoons olive oil
3 garlic cloves, crushed
1 small red chilli, finely chopped
  (see NOTE)
800 g (1 lb 12 oz) tinned chopped tomatoes
30 g (1 oz/⅓ cup) grated pecorino cheese

1 Bring a large saucepan of salted water to the boil and cook the pasta and potato together for 8–10 minutes, or until the pasta is *al dente*. Drain and return to the saucepan. Meanwhile, trim the broccoli into florets and discard the stems. Place in a saucepan of boiling water and cook for 1–2 minutes, then drain and plunge into iced water. Drain and add to the cooked pasta and potato.

2 Heat the oil in a saucepan, add the garlic and chilli and cook for 30 seconds. Add the tomato and simmer for 5 minutes, or until slightly reduced and thickened. Season to taste with salt and freshly ground black pepper.

3 Pour the tomato mixture over the pasta, potato and broccoli. Toss well and stir over low heat until warmed through. Serve sprinkled with grated pecorino cheese.

NOTE: *Wearing rubber gloves when chopping or seeding chillies will help to avoid skin irritation.*

Blanch the broccoli in boiling water for a couple of minutes then cool in iced water.

Simmer the tomato sauce for 5 minutes or until it has thickened.

NUTRITION PER SERVE
Protein 20 g; Fat 22 g; Carbohydrate 77 g; Dietary Fibre 11 g; Cholesterol 6 mg; 2445 kJ (585 Cal)

Pasta shells with walnut pesto

PREPARATION TIME: 15 MINUTES | TOTAL COOKING TIME: 15 MINUTES | SERVES 4–6

125 g (4½ oz) day-old crusty bread, crusts
    removed
185 g (6½ oz/1½ cups) walnut pieces
500 g (1 lb 2 oz) pasta shells
1 very large handful basil, roughly chopped
2–3 garlic cloves, peeled
1 small red chilli, seeded and roughly chopped
    (see NOTE)
½ teaspoon finely grated lemon zest
3 tablespoons lemon juice
125 ml (4 fl oz/½ cup) olive oil

1 Preheat the oven to 160°C (315°F/Gas 2–3). Cut the bread into 2 cm (¾ inch) thick slices and place on a baking tray with the walnuts. Bake for 8–10 minutes, or until the bread is dried out a little and the walnuts are lightly toasted. Don't overcook the walnuts or they will become bitter.

2 Meanwhile, cook the pasta in a large saucepan of rapidly boiling salted water until *al dente*. Drain well and return to the pan to keep warm.

3 Break the bread into chunks and mix in a food processor with the walnuts, basil, garlic, chilli, lemon zest and juice. Use the pulse button to chop the mixture without forming a paste. Transfer to a bowl and stir in the oil. Toss through the pasta, then season to taste with salt and pepper.

HINT: *Don't add the oil to the food processor or the pesto will lose its crunchy texture.*

NOTE: *Wearing rubber gloves when chopping or seeding chillies will help to avoid skin irritation*

NUTRITION PER SERVE (6)
Protein 15 g; Fat 39 g; Carbohydrate 70 g; Dietary Fibre 7 g; Cholesterol 0 mg; 2870 kJ (685 Cal)

Bake the bread and the walnuts on the same tray to dry out the bread and lightly toast the nuts.

Transfer the mixture to a bowl before stirring in the oil.

Cotelli with spring vegetables

PREPARATION TIME: 15 MINUTES | TOTAL COOKING TIME: 20 MINUTES | SERVES 4

500 g (1 lb 2 oz) cotelli
310 g (11 oz/2 cups) frozen peas
310 g (11 oz/2 cups) frozen broad (fava) beans
4 tablespoons olive oil
6 spring onions (scallions), cut into short pieces
2 garlic cloves, finely chopped
250 ml (9 fl oz/1 cup) chicken stock
12 asparagus spears, chopped
1 lemon
parmesan shaved, to serve

NUTRITION PER SERVE
Protein 25 g; Fat 21 g; Carbohydrate 103 g; Dietary Fibre 19 g; Cholesterol 0 mg; 2935 kJ (700 Cal)

1 Cook the pasta in a large saucepan of rapidly boiling salted water until *al dente.* Drain well and return to the pan to keep warm.

2 Meanwhile, cook the peas in a saucepan of boiling water for 1–2 minutes, or until tender. Remove with a slotted spoon and plunge into cold water. Add the broad beans to the same saucepan of boiling water and cook for 1–2 minutes, then drain and plunge into cold water. Remove and slip out of their skins.

3 Heat 2 tablespoons of the oil in a frying pan. Add the spring onion and garlic and cook over medium heat for 2 minutes, or until softened. Pour in the stock and cook for 5 minutes, or until slightly reduced. Add the asparagus and cook for 3–4 minutes, or until bright green and just tender. Stir in the peas and broad beans and cook for 2–3 minutes to heat through.

4 Toss the remaining oil through the pasta, then add the vegetable mixture, ½ teaspoon finely grated lemon zest and 3 tablespoons of lemon juice. Season and toss together well. Serve with shaved parmesan.

Blanch the broad beans in boiling water then iced water and then slip the beans out of their skins.

Add the asparagus to the pan and cook until bright green and just tender.

Toss the pasta and vegetables together, then add the lemon zest and juice.

Pasta with rocket and mushrooms

PREPARATION TIME: 15 MINUTES + 10 MINUTES SOAKING | TOTAL COOKING TIME: 15 MINUTES | SERVES 4

15 g (½ oz) dried porcini mushrooms
375 g (13 oz) pasta
1 tablespoon salted butter
3 tablespoons extra virgin olive oil
2 garlic cloves, crushed
250 g (9 oz) button mushrooms, sliced
3 tablespoons lemon juice
30 g (1 oz) grated parmesan cheese
90 g (3¼ oz) baby rocket (arugula) leaves

1   Soak the porcini mushrooms in 4 tablespoons boiling water for 10 minutes to soften. Cook the pasta in a large saucepan of rapidly boiling salted water until *al dente*. Drain well and return to the pan to keep warm.

2   Meanwhile, heat the butter and oil over medium heat in a frying pan. Add the garlic and button mushrooms and cook for 4 minutes, tossing occasionally. Drain the porcini mushrooms, reserving the soaking liquid. Chop all of the mushrooms, then add them to the frying pan with the soaking liquid. Bring to a simmer.

3   Add the mushroom mixture, lemon juice and parmesan to the saucepan with the pasta and toss together. Season to taste with salt and freshly ground black pepper. Toss through the rocket just before serving.

Soak the porcini mushrooms in boiling water to soften them.

Cook the garlic and button mushrooms for 4 minutes before adding the porcini.

NUTRITION PER SERVE
Protein 16 g; Fat 23 g; Carbohydrate 68 g; Dietary Fibre 7 g; Cholesterol 22 mg; 2265 kJ (540 Cal)

Potato gnocchi with tomato-olive sauce

PREPARATION TIME: 10 MINUTES I TOTAL COOKING TIME: 15 MINUTES I SERVES 4

500 g (1 lb 2 oz) fresh potato gnocchi
2 tablespoons oil
1 leek, sliced
250 ml (9 fl oz/1 cup) bottled tomato pasta
    sauce
170 ml (5½ fl oz/⅔ cup) vegetable stock
60 g (2¼ oz) chopped black olives
6 anchovies, chopped

1   Cook the gnocchi in a large saucepan
of rapidly boiling salted water until they float to
the surface. Lift out with a slotted spoon.

2   Meanwhile, heat the oil in a large saucepan
and add the leek. Stir over medium heat for
2 minutes or until tender. Add the tomato
pasta sauce, stock, olives and anchovy and
stir for 5 minutes to heat through. Serve over
the gnocchi.

STORAGE: *The sauce will keep for a day,
covered, in the refrigerator.*

NOTE: *Fresh potato gnocchi is available from
supermarkets and delicatessens. Use any other
dried or fresh pasta if you prefer.*

NUTRITION PER SERVE
Protein 6 g; Fat 11 g; Carbohydrate 25 g; Dietary
Fibre 5 g; Cholesterol 2 mg; 930 kJ (222 Cal)

Add the tomato pasta sauce, stock, olives and
anchovy to the leek and heat through.

Spaghetti with herbs, baby spinach and garlic crumbs

PREPARATION TIME: 15 MINUTES | TOTAL COOKING TIME: 15 MINUTES | SERVES 4

375 g (13 oz) spaghetti
125 g (4½ oz) day-old crusty Italian bread,
   crusts removed
100 ml (3½ fl oz) extra virgin olive oil, plus
   extra for serving
4 garlic cloves, finely chopped
400 g (14 oz) baby English spinach leaves
4 tablespoons chopped basil
2 large handfuls chopped flat-leaf (Italian)
   parsley
1 tablespoon thyme leaves
30 g (1 oz) shaved parmesan cheese, to serve

NUTRITION PER SERVE
Protein 19 g; Fat 23.5 g; Carbohydrate 82 g; Dietary
Fibre 9 g; Cholesterol 7 mg; 2590 kJ (620 Cal)

1   Cook the pasta in a large saucepan of
rapidly boiling salted water until *al dente*.
Drain well and return to the pan to keep
warm, reserving 125 ml (4 fl oz/½ cup) of
the cooking water.

2   To make the garlic breadcrumbs, mix the
bread in a food processor or blender until
coarse crumbs form. Heat 1 tablespoon of
oil in a saucepan. Add the breadcrumbs and
half the garlic and toss for 2–3 minutes, or
until lightly golden. Remove and clean the
pan with paper towels.

3   Heat 2 tablespoons of the oil in the same
pan. Add the spinach and remaining garlic,
toss together for 1 minute, then add the herbs.
Cook, tossing frequently, for a further 1 minute
to wilt the herbs a little and to heat through.
Toss through the pasta with the remaining oil
and reserved pasta water. Divide among serving
bowls and scatter with the garlic breadcrumbs.
Serve hot sprinkled with parmesan and drizzled
with extra virgin olive oil.

Cook the spaghetti until *al dente*, then drain and return to the pan to keep warm.

Cook the breadcrumbs and half the garlic until lightly golden.

Add the spinach and remaining garlic to the oil in the pan and toss together over the heat.

Cavatelli with herb sauce and pecorino

PREPARATION TIME: 10 MINUTES | TOTAL COOKING TIME: 20 MINUTES | SERVES 4

400 g (14 oz) cavatelli
90 g (3¼ oz) salted butter
2 garlic cloves, crushed
3 tablespoons snipped chives
3 tablespoons shredded basil
1 tablespoon shredded sage
1 teaspoon thyme
3 tablespoons warm vegetable stock
60 g (2¼ oz) pecorino cheese, grated
sage leaves, to serve

1   Cook the pasta in a large saucepan of rapidly boiling salted water until *al dente*. Drain well and return to the pan to keep warm. Meanwhile, heat the butter in a small saucepan over medium heat, add the garlic and cook for 1 minute, or until fragrant. Add the chives, basil, sage and thyme and cook for a further minute.

2   Add the herb mixture and stock to the pasta in the pan. Return to the heat for 2–3 minutes, or until warmed through. Season to taste, add the pecorino and stir well. Divide among bowls and garnish with sage leaves.

NOTE: *Pecorino is Italian sheep's milk cheese with a sharp flavour. If you can't find it, use parmesan instead.*

Add the chives, basil, sage and thyme to the sauce and cook for another minute.

Add the herb sauce and the stock to the pasta and return to the heat.

NUTRITION PER SERVE
Protein 16 g; Fat 22 g; Carbohydrate 71 g; Dietary Fibre 6 g; Cholesterol 65 mg; 2280 kJ (545 Cal)

Fettuccine with creamy spinach and roast tomato

PREPARATION TIME: 10 MINUTES | TOTAL COOKING TIME: 35 MINUTES | SERVES 4–6

6 roma (plum) tomatoes
2 tablespoons salted butter
2 garlic cloves, crushed
1 onion, chopped
500 g (1 lb 2 oz) English spinach
250 ml (9 fl oz/1 cup) vegetable stock
125 ml (4 fl oz/½ cup) thickened (whipping)
   cream
500 g (1 lb 2 oz) fresh spinach fettuccine
60 g (2¼ oz) grated parmesan cheese

1 Preheat the oven to 220°C (425°F/Gas 7). Cut the tomatoes in half lengthways, then cut each half into three wedges. Place the wedges on a lightly greased baking tray and bake for 30–35 minutes, or until softened and slightly golden. Meanwhile, heat the butter in a large frying pan. Add the garlic and onion and cook over medium heat for 5 minutes, or until the onion is soft. Add the spinach, stock and cream, increase the heat to high and bring to the boil. Simmer rapidly for 5 minutes then season well and process in a food processor until smooth.

2 Meanwhile, cook the pasta in a large saucepan of rapidly boiling salted water until *al dente*. Drain well and return to the pan to keep warm. Toss with the spinach sauce. Divide among serving bowls and top with the roasted tomatoes and parmesan.

Add the spinach, stock and cream to the sauce and simmer rapidly.

Transfer the spinach sauce to a food processor and mix until smooth.

NUTRITION PER SERVE (6)
Protein 17 g; Fat 18 g; Carbohydrate 65 g; Dietary Fibre 8 g; Cholesterol 49 mg; 2035 kJ (485 Cal)

Fusilli with mushroom and herb sauce

PREPARATION TIME: 15 MINUTES | TOTAL COOKING TIME: 25 MINUTES | SERVES 4

2 tablespoons olive oil

500 g (1 lb 2 oz) button mushrooms, sliced

2 garlic cloves, crushed

2 teaspoons chopped marjoram

125 ml (4 fl oz/½ cup) dry white wine

4 tablespoons pouring (whipping) cream

375 g (13 oz) fusilli

1 tablespoon lemon juice

1 teaspoon finely grated lemon zest

2 tablespoons chopped parsley

60 g (2¼ oz) grated parmesan cheese

NUTRITION PER SERVE
Protein 20 g; Fat 18 g; Carbohydrate 67 g; Dietary Fibre 6.5 g; Cholesterol 25 mg; 2275 kJ (545 Cal)

1 Heat the oil in a large heavy-based frying pan over high heat. Add the mushrooms and cook for 3 minutes, stirring constantly. Add the garlic and marjoram and cook for 2 minutes.

2 Add the wine, reduce the heat and simmer for 5 minutes, or until nearly all the liquid has evaporated. Stir in the cream and continue to cook over low heat for 5 minutes, or until the sauce has thickened.

3 Meanwhile, cook the pasta in a large saucepan of rapidly boiling salted water until *al dente*. Drain well and return to the pan to keep warm.

4 Add the lemon juice, zest, parsley and half the parmesan to the sauce. Season to taste. Toss the penne through the sauce and sprinkle with the remaining parmesan.

Add the garlic and marjoram to the softened mushrooms and cook for another 2 minutes.

Stir the lemon juice, zest, parsley and the parmesan into the sauce.

Free-form wild mushroom lasagne

PREPARATION TIME: 10 MINUTES + 15 MINUTES SOAKING | TOTAL COOKING TIME: 15 MINUTES | SERVES 4

10 g (¼ oz) dried porcini mushrooms
350 g (12 oz) wild mushrooms (such as
 shiitake, oyster, Swiss brown)
30 g (1 oz) salted butter
1 small onion, halved and thinly sliced
1 tablespoon chopped thyme
3 egg yolks
125 ml (4 fl oz/½ cup) thickened (whipping)
 cream
100 g (3½ oz/1 cup) grated parmesan cheese
8 fresh lasagne sheets (10 x 25 cm/
 4 x 10 inches)

1 Soak the porcini in 3 tablespoons boiling water for 15 minutes. Strain through a sieve, reserving the liquid. Cut the larger of all the mushrooms in half. Heat the butter in a frying pan and cook the onion over medium heat for 1–2 minutes, or until just soft. Add the thyme and mushrooms (including the porcini) and cook for 1–2 minutes, or until softened. Pour in the reserved mushroom liquid and cook for 1–2 minutes, or until the liquid has evaporated. Set aside.

2 Beat the egg yolks, cream and half the parmesan in a large bowl. Cook the lasagne sheets in a large saucepan of boiling water for 2–3 minutes, stirring gently. Drain well and toss the sheets gently through the egg mixture while hot. Reheat the mushrooms quickly. To serve, place a sheet of folded lasagne on a plate, top with some mushrooms, then another sheet of folded lasagne. Drizzle with any remaining egg mixture and sprinkle with the remaining parmesan.

Add the thyme and all the mushrooms to the pan, then add the porcini soaking liquid.

Toss the lasagne sheets gently though the egg, cream and parmesan mixture.

NUTRITION PER SERVE
Protein 20 g; Fat 30 g; Carbohydrate 30 g; Dietary Fibre 4.5 g; Cholesterol 213 mg; 1950 kJ (465 Cal)

Blue cheese and walnut lasagnette

PREPARATION TIME: **10** MINUTES | TOTAL COOKING TIME: **15** MINUTES | SERVES **4**

375 g (13 oz) lasagnette
100 g (3½ oz/1 cup) walnuts
2 tablespoons salted butter
3 French shallots (eschalots), finely chopped
1 tablespoon brandy
250 ml (9 fl oz/1 cup) crème fraîche
200 g (7 oz) gorgonzola cheese, crumbled
    (see NOTE)
75 g (2½ oz) baby English spinach

1 Preheat the oven to 200°C (400°F/Gas 6). Cook the pasta in a large saucepan of rapidly boiling salted water until *al dente*. Drain well and return to the pan to keep warm. Meanwhile, place the walnuts on a baking tray and roast for 5 minutes, or until golden and toasted. Cool, then roughly chop.

2 Heat the butter in a large saucepan, add the shallots and cook over medium heat for 1–2 minutes, or until soft but not brown. Add the brandy and simmer for 1 minute. Stir in the crème fraîche and gorgonzola. Cook for 3–4 minutes, or until the cheese has melted and the sauce has thickened. Stir in the spinach and walnuts, reserving 1 tablespoon of walnuts to garnish. Heat gently until the spinach has just wilted. Season and gently mix the sauce through the pasta. Sprinkle with the reserved walnuts to serve.

NOTE: *Use young gorgonzola that has a sweeter, milder flavour than mature.*

Roast the walnuts in the oven until they are golden, then roughly chop.

Cook the sauce until the cheese has melted and the sauce has thickened.

NUTRITION PER SERVE
Protein 32 g; Fat 64 g; Carbohydrate 69 g; Dietary Fibre 4.5 g; Cholesterol 152 mg; 4095 kJ (980 Cal)

Filled pasta

Chicken agnolotti

PREPARATION TIME: 45 MINUTES + 30 MINUTES STANDING | TOTAL COOKING TIME: 45 MINUTES | SERVES 4

PASTA
250 g (9 oz/2 cups) plain (all-purpose) flour
3 eggs
1 tablespoon olive oil
1 egg yolk, extra

FILLING
125 g (4½ oz) minced (ground) chicken
75 g (2½ oz) ricotta or cottage cheese
60 g (2¼ oz) chicken livers, trimmed and
    chopped
30 g (1 oz) prosciutto, chopped
1 slice salami, chopped
2 tablespoons grated parmesan cheese
1 egg, beaten
1 tablespoon chopped parsley
1 garlic clove, crushed
¼ teaspoon mixed (pumpkin pie) spice

TOMATO SAUCE
2 tablespoons olive oil
1 onion, finely chopped
2 garlic cloves, crushed
850 g (1 lb 14 oz) tinned chopped tomatoes
1 handful chopped basil
½ teaspoon mixed herbs

NUTRITION PER SERVE
Protein 30 g; Fat 25 g; Carbohydrate 60 g; Dietary
Fibre 6 g; Cholesterol 223 mg; 2534 kJ (605 Cal)

1 To make the pasta, sift the flour and a pinch of salt onto a board. Make a well in the centre of the flour. In a bowl, whisk together the eggs, oil and 1 tablespoon water. Add the egg mixture gradually to flour, working in with your hands until mixture forms a ball. Knead on a lightly floured surface for 5 minutes, or until smooth and elastic. Place the dough in a lightly oiled bowl and cover with plastic wrap. Allow to stand for 30 minutes.

2 To make the filling, process all filling ingredients in processor until finely chopped.

3 To make the sauce, heat the oil in a saucepan. Add the onion and garlic and stir over low heat until onion is tender. Increase heat, add tomatoes, basil, herbs and season. Stir. Bring to the boil. Reduce heat and simmer for 15 minutes. Remove from the heat.

4 Roll out half the dough until 1 mm (¹⁄₁₆ inch) thick. Cut into 10 cm (4 inch) strips. Place teaspoons of filling at 5 cm (2 inch) intervals down one side of each strip. Whisk together extra egg yolk and 3 tablespoons water. Brush along one side of dough and between the filling. Fold dough over filling. Press edges together. Cut between the mounds of filling with a knife or a fluted pastry cutter.

5 Cook ravioli in batches in rapidly boiling salted water for 10 minutes. Reheat the sauce in a large pan. Add the cooked ravioli and toss well until the sauce is evenly distributed. Simmer, stirring, for 5 minutes, then serve.

Knead the pasta mixture on a lightly floured surface until smooth and elastic.

Place teaspoons of the filling at 5 cm (2 inch) intervals down one side of each strip.

Use a fluted pastry cutter or knife to cut between the mounds of filling.

Veal tortellini with creamy mushroom sauce

PREPARATION TIME: 15 MINUTES | TOTAL COOKING TIME: 20 MINUTES | SERVES 4

500 g (1 lb 2 oz) veal tortellini

3 tablespoons olive oil

600 g (1 lb 5 oz) Swiss brown mushrooms, thinly sliced

2 garlic cloves, crushed

125 ml (4 fl oz/½ cup) dry white wine

300 ml (10½ fl oz) thickened (whipping) cream

pinch of grated nutmeg

3 tablespoons finely chopped flat-leaf (Italian) parsley

30 g (1 oz) grated parmesan cheese, to serve

1 Cook the pasta in a large saucepan of rapidly boiling salted water until *al dente.* Drain well and return to the pan to keep warm. Meanwhile, heat the oil in a frying pan over medium heat. Add the mushrooms and cook, stirring occasionally and gently, for 5 minutes, or until softened. Add the garlic and cook for 1 minute, then stir in the wine and cook for 5 minutes, or until the liquid has reduced by half.

2 Add the cream, nutmeg and parsley, stir to combine and cook for 3–5 minutes, or until the sauce thickens slightly. Season with salt and freshly ground black pepper. Divide the tortellini among four serving plates and spoon on the mushroom sauce. Sprinkle with parmesan cheese (if desired) and serve.

Heat the oil in a frying pan, add the mushrooms and cook until softened.

Add the cream, nutmeg and parsley and stir until the sauce thickens slightly.

NUTRITION PER SERVE
Protein 24 g; Fat 53 g; Carbohydrate 50 g; Dietary Fibre 8.5 g; Cholesterol 125 mg; 3275 kJ (785 Cal)

Ravioli with herbs

PREPARATION TIME: 5 MINUTES | TOTAL COOKING TIME: 15 MINUTES | SERVES 4–6

2 tablespoons olive oil
1 garlic clove, halved
800 g (1 lb 12 oz) ravioli
60 g (2¼ oz) salted butter, chopped
2 tablespoons chopped parsley
1 large handful chopped basil
2 tablespoons snipped chives

1 Combine the oil and garlic in a small bowl and set aside. Cook the pasta in a large saucepan of rapidly boiling salted water until *al dente*. Drain well and return to the pan to keep warm.

2 Add the oil to the pasta, discarding the garlic. Add the butter and herbs and toss well before serving.

VARIATION: *Use fresh coriander (cilantro) instead of parsley.*

NUTRITION PER SERVE (6)
Protein 10 g; Fat 21 g; Carbohydrate 19 g; Dietary Fibre 2 g; Cholesterol 48 mg; 1271 kJ (304 Cal)

Add the oil to the cooked pasta and then add the butter and herbs and toss well.

Chicken tortellini with tomato sauce

PREPARATION TIME: 30 MINUTES + 30 MINUTES RESTING | TOTAL COOKING TIME: 30 MINUTES | SERVES 4

PASTA
250 g (9 oz/2 cups) plain (all-purpose) flour
3 eggs
1 tablespoon olive oil

FILLING
20 g (¾ oz) salted butter
80 g (2¾ oz) boneless, skinless chicken
    breast, cubed
2 slices pancetta, chopped
50 g (1¾ oz/½ cup) grated parmesan cheese
½ teaspoon nutmeg
1 egg, lightly beaten

TOMATO SAUCE
4 tablespoons olive oil
1.5 kg (3 lb 5 oz) ripe tomatoes, peeled and
    chopped
1 large handful chopped oregano
50 g (1¾ oz/½ cup) grated parmesan cheese

100 g (3½ oz) fresh bocconcini (fresh baby
    mozzarella cheese), thinly sliced, to serve

NUTRITION PER SERVE
Protein 33 g; Fat 44 g; Carbohydrate 53 g; Dietary
Fibre 7 g; Cholesterol 230 mg; 3090 kJ (740 Cal)

1 To make the pasta, sift the flour and a pinch of salt into a bowl. Make a well in the centre. In a bowl, whisk together the eggs, oil and 1 tablespoon water. Add gradually to the flour, mixing to a firm dough. Make a ball, adding a little extra water if necessary. Knead on a lightly floured surface for 5 minutes, or until the dough is elastic. Place in a lightly oiled bowl, cover with plastic wrap. Leave for 30 minutes.

2 To make the filling, heat the butter in a frying pan, add the chicken and cook until golden brown. Drain. Process the chicken and pancetta in a food processor until finely chopped. Transfer to a bowl and add the cheese, nutmeg and egg. Set aside.

3 Roll out dough very thinly on a lightly floured surface. Using a floured cutter, cut into 5 cm (2 inch) rounds. Spoon about ½ teaspoon of filling into the centre of each round. Fold the rounds in half to form semi-circles, pressing the edges together firmly. Wrap each semi-circle around your finger to form a ring and then press the ends of the dough together firmly.

4 To make the sauce, place the oil, tomato and oregano in a frying pan and cook over high heat for 10 minutes. Stir in the parmesan. Set aside.

5 Cook the tortellini in two batches in rapidly boiling water for about 6 minutes for each batch. Drain well and return to the pan. Reheat the sauce, add to tortellini and toss to combine. Divide the tortellini among individual bowls, top with the bocconcini and allow the cheese to melt a little before serving.

Roll out the dough very thinly and cut into rounds with a floured pastry cutter.

Add the cheese, nutmeg and egg to the processed filling mixture.

Wrap the semi-circles around your finger to make a ring and press the ends together.

Beetroot ravioli with sage burnt butter

PREPARATION TIME: 15 MINUTES I TOTAL COOKING TIME: 15 MINUTES I SERVES 4

340 g (11¾ oz) jar baby beetroots (beets) in
    sweet vinegar
40 g (1½ oz) grated parmesan cheese
250 g (9 oz/1 cup) ricotta cheese
750 g (1 lb 10 oz) fresh lasagne sheets
fine cornmeal, for sprinkling
200 g (7 oz) salted butter, chopped
8 sage leaves, torn
2 garlic cloves, crushed

1   Drain the beetroot, then grate it into a bowl.
Add the parmesan cheese and ricotta and mix
well. Lay a sheet of pasta on a flat surface and
place evenly spaced tablespoons of the beetroot
mixture on the pasta to give 12 mounds—four
across and three down. Flatten the mounds
slightly. Lightly brush the edges of the pasta
sheet and around each pile of filling with water.

2   Place a second sheet of pasta over the top
and gently press around each mound to seal and
enclose the filling. Using a fluted pastry cutter
or sharp knife, cut the pasta into 12 ravioli. Lay
them out separately on a lined tray that has been
sprinkled with the cornmeal. Repeat with the
remaining filling and lasagne sheets to make
24 ravioli. Gently remove any excess air bubbles
after cutting so that they are completely sealed.

3   Cook the pasta in a large saucepan of rapidly
boiling salted water until *al dente*. Drain well and
return to the pan to keep warm. Melt the butter
in a saucepan and cook for 3–4 minutes, or until
golden brown. Remove from the heat, stir in
the sage and garlic and spoon over the ravioli.
Sprinkle with shaved parmesan to serve.

Brush between the mounds of filling with a little
water so the pasta will stick.

Remove the melted butter from the heat and stir in
the sage and garlic.

NUTRITION PER SERVE
Protein 16 g; Fat 52 g; Carbohydrate 33 g; Dietary
Fibre 3 g; Cholesterol 168 mg; 2720 kJ (650 Cal)

Spinach and ricotta shells

PREPARATION TIME: 15 MINUTES | TOTAL COOKING TIME: 15 MINUTES | SERVES 4

20 conchiglie (large pasta shells)
1 tablespoon olive oil
2 bacon slices, finely chopped
1 onion, finely chopped
500 g (1 lb 2 oz) English spinach, chopped
750 g (1 lb 10 oz/3 cups) ricotta cheese
30 g (1 oz/⅓ cup) grated parmesan cheese
250 ml (9 fl oz/1 cup) bottled tomato pasta
    sauce
toasted pine nuts, for serving

1   Cook the pasta in a large saucepan of rapidly boiling salted water until *al dente.* Drain well. Meanwhile, heat the oil in a frying pan and cook the bacon and onion over medium heat for 3 minutes or until lightly browned. Add the spinach and stir over low heat until wilted. Add the ricotta and stir until combined.

2   Spoon the filling into the pasta shells and sprinkle with parmesan cheese. Place on a cold, lightly oiled grill tray and grill (broil) under medium-high heat for 3 minutes or until lightly browned and heated through.

3   Heat the tomato pasta sauce in a small saucepan for 1 minute or until heated through. Spoon the sauce onto serving plates and top with the filled shells. Sprinkle with pine nuts to serve.

STORAGE: *The shells can be filled several hours before required. Store, covered, in the refrigerator and grill just before serving.*

Cook the bacon and onion until lightly browned, then add the spinach and stir until wilted.

Spoon the filling into the cooked pasta shells and then sprinkle with parmesan.

NUTRITION PER SERVE
Protein 33 g; Fat 31 g; Carbohydrate 37 g; Dietary Fibre 4 g; Cholesterol 109 mg; 2344 kJ (560 Cal)

Tortellini with speck, asparagus and tomato

PREPARATION TIME: 15 MINUTES | TOTAL COOKING TIME: 15 MINUTES | SERVES 4–6

200 g (7 oz) piece speck (skin removed if it
   has one)
4 tomatoes
300 g (10½ oz) asparagus spears, cut into
   short lengths
500 g (1 lb 2 oz) cheese tortellini
1 tablespoon olive oil
1 red onion, thinly sliced
1 tablespoon tomato paste (concentrated
   purée)
125 ml (4 fl oz/½ cup) chicken stock
2 teaspoons thyme leaves

NUTRITION PER SERVE (6)
Protein 22 g; Fat 18 g; Carbohydrate 25 g; Dietary
Fibre 5 g; Cholesterol 53 mg; 1455 kJ (345 Cal)

1   Chop the speck in a food processor. Score
a cross in the base of each tomato, place in a
heatproof bowl and cover with boiling water.
Leave for 1 minute, then plunge into cold water
and peel the skin away from the cross. Roughly
chop the tomatoes.

2   Cook the asparagus in a large saucepan of
boiling water for 2 minutes, or until just tender,
then remove and refresh in cold water. Drain.
Cook the pasta in a large saucepan of rapidly
boiling salted water until *al dente*. Drain well
and return to the pan to keep warm.

3   Meanwhile, heat the oil in a saucepan, add
the speck and onion and cook, stirring, over
medium heat for 2–3 minutes, or until the
onion is soft. Add the tomato, tomato paste,
stock and thyme and season to taste with
salt and freshly ground black pepper. Cook,
stirring, for 5 minutes. Add the pasta and
asparagus to the tomato mixture and stir over
low heat until warmed through. Divide among
warmed bowls and serve.

Remove skin from speck if it has one. Chop the speck in a food processor using the pulse button.

Blanch the asparagus in hot and then cold water so it keeps its bright colour.

Add the tomato, tomato paste, stock and thyme and simmer the sauce for 5 minutes.

Agnolotti with salmon, capers and brown butter

PREPARATION TIME: 10 MINUTES | TOTAL COOKING TIME: 20 MINUTES | SERVES 4

125 ml (4 fl oz/½ cup) olive oil
100 g (3½ oz) capers, drained and rinsed,
    patted dry
500 g (1 lb 2 oz) salmon fillets, skinned
625 g (1 lb 6 oz) ricotta agnolotti
150 g (5½ oz) salted butter
1½ teaspoons grated lemon zest
2 tablespoons lemon juice
3 tablespoons chopped parsley

1 Heat half the oil in a small frying pan and cook the capers over high heat for 3–4 minutes, until golden and crispy. Drain on paper towels.

2 Season the salmon fillets on both sides with salt and pepper. Heat the remaining oil in a non-stick frying pan and cook the salmon for 2–3 minutes each side, or until just cooked through but still pink in the centre. Remove from the pan and keep warm. Flake with your fingers.

3 Cook the pasta in a large saucepan of rapidly boiling salted water until *al dente*. Drain well and return to the pan to keep warm. Heat the butter in a frying pan over low heat for 5 minutes, or until golden. Add the lemon zest, juice and parsley. Top the pasta with the flaked salmon and pour on the brown butter. Scatter with the capers and serve immediately.

NUTRITION PER SERVE
Protein 36 g; Fat 68 g; Carbohydrate 44 g; Dietary Fibre 5 g; Cholesterol 181 mg; 3865 kJ (925 Cal)

Pat the capers dry before frying them in the hot oil or they will spit.

Flake the salmon into pieces with your fingers, removing any bones as you go.

Heat the butter until golden, then add the lemon zest, lemon juice and parsley.

Veal tortellini with baked pumpkin and basil butter

PREPARATION TIME: 15 MINUTES | TOTAL COOKING TIME: 30 MINUTES | SERVES 4

1 kg (2 lb 4 oz) jap or kent pumpkin (winter squash), cut into 2 cm (¾ inch) cubes
600 g (1 lb 5 oz) veal tortellini with cracked pepper
100 g (3½ oz) salted butter
3 garlic cloves, crushed
90 g (3¼ oz) pine nuts
2 large handfuls shredded basil
200 g (7 oz) crumbled feta cheese

1   Preheat the oven to 220°C (425°F/Gas 7). Line a baking tray with baking paper. Place the pumpkin on the prepared tray and season well with salt and freshly ground black pepper. Bake for 30 minutes, or until the pumpkin is tender.

2   Meanwhile, cook the pasta in a large saucepan of rapidly boiling salted water until *al dente*. Drain well and return to the pan to keep warm.

3   Heat the butter over medium heat in a small frying pan until foaming. Add the garlic and pine nuts and cook for 3–5 minutes, or until the nuts are starting to turn golden. Remove from the heat and add the basil. Toss the basil butter, pumpkin and feta through the cooked pasta and serve immediately.

NUTRITION PER SERVE
Protein 34 g; Fat 57 g; Carbohydrate 72 g; Dietary Fibre 10 g; Cholesterol 136.5 mg; 3900 kJ (930 Cal)

Place the pumpkin on a baking tray and roast for 30 minutes.

Heat the butter until foaming and then add the garlic and pine nuts.

Herb-filled ravioli

PREPARATION TIME: 1 HOUR + 30 MINUTES STANDING | TOTAL COOKING TIME: 10 MINUTES | SERVES 4

300 g (10½ oz) plain (all-purpose) flour

3 eggs, beaten

3 tablespoons olive oil

250 g (9 oz/1 cup) ricotta cheese

2 tablespoons grated parmesan cheese

2 teaspoons snipped chives

1 tablespoon chopped flat-leaf (Italian) parsley

2 teaspoons chopped basil

1 teaspoon chopped lemon thyme or thyme

1 egg, beaten, extra

NUTRITION PER SERVE
Protein 25 g; Fat 30 g; Carbohydrate 55 g; Dietary Fibre 3 g; Cholesterol 215 mg; 2395 kJ (570 Cal)

1 Sift the flour into a bowl and make a well in the centre. Gradually mix in the eggs and oil. Turn out onto a lightly floured surface and knead for 6 minutes, or until elastic. Cover with plastic wrap and leave for 30 minutes.

2 To make the filling, mix the ricotta, parmesan and herbs. Season well.

3 Divide the dough into four portions and shape each into a log. Keep unworked portions covered. Take one portion and flatten with a rolling pin. Roll out each portion as thinly as possible into rectangles, making 2 slightly larger and wider than the others.

4 Spread one of the smaller sheets out. Spoon 1 teaspoon of the filling at 5 cm (2 inch) intervals. Brush the egg between the filling along the cutting lines. Place a larger sheet on top. Press the two sheets together along the cutting lines. Cut the ravioli with a pastry cutter or knife. Transfer to a lightly floured baking tray. Repeat with the remaining sheets and filling. Cook the ravioli in a large saucepan of rapidly boiling water for 5–8 minutes and top with a sauce of your choice.

Mix together the ricotta, parmesan and herbs and season with salt and pepper.

Brush the beaten egg between the filling along the cutting lines.

Ham tortellini with nutty herb sauce

PREPARATION TIME: 15 MINUTES | TOTAL COOKING TIME: 15 MINUTES | SERVES 4–6

500 g (1 lb 2 oz) ham and cheese tortellini
60 g (2¼ oz) salted butter
125 g (4½ oz/1 cup) walnuts, chopped
100 g (3½ oz/⅔ cup) pine nuts
2 tablespoons finely chopped flat-leaf (Italian) parsley
2 teaspoons chopped thyme
60 g (2¼ oz/¼ cup) ricotta cheese
3 tablespoons pouring (whipping) cream

1 Cook the pasta in a large saucepan of rapidly boiling salted water until *al dente*. Drain well and return to the pan to keep warm. Meanwhile, heat the butter in a frying pan over medium heat until foaming. Add the walnuts and pine nuts and stir for 5 minutes, or until golden brown. Add the parsley and thyme and season to taste.

2 Beat the ricotta and cream together. Add the nutty sauce to the pasta and toss. Divide among serving bowls and top with the ricotta cream.

NUTRITION PER SERVE (6)
Protein 22 g; Fat 47 g; Carbohydrate 23 g; Dietary Fibre 4 g; Cholesterol 85 mg; 2495 kJ (595 Cal)

Heat the butter until foaming and then cook the walnuts and pine nuts until golden.

Agnolotti with creamy tomato sauce and bacon

PREPARATION TIME: 10 MINUTES | TOTAL COOKING TIME: 20 MINUTES | SERVES 4

4 bacon slices

625 g (1 lb 6 oz) veal or chicken agnolotti

1 tablespoon olive oil

2 garlic cloves, finely chopped

120 g (4¼ oz/¾ cup) semi-dried (sun-blushed) tomatoes, thinly sliced

1 tablespoon chopped thyme

375 ml (13 fl oz/1½ cups) pouring (whipping) cream

1 teaspoon finely grated lemon zest

30 g (1 oz) grated parmesan cheese

1 Grill (broil) the bacon for 5 minutes on each side, or until crisp and golden. Drain on paper towels and then break into pieces.

2 Cook the pasta in a large saucepan of rapidly boiling salted water until *al dente*. Drain well and return to the pan to keep warm. Heat the oil in a frying pan and cook the garlic over medium heat for 1 minute, or until just golden. Add the tomato and thyme and cook for 1 minute.

3 Add the cream, bring to the boil, then reduce the heat and simmer for 6–8 minutes, or until thickened and reduced by one-third. Season with salt and pepper and add the lemon zest and 2 tablespoons of the parmesan cheese. Serve over the pasta, topped with the remaining parmesan cheese (if desired) and bacon pieces. Serve immediately.

Grill the bacon until it is crisp, then drain on paper towels and break into pieces.

Add the semi-dried tomatoes and thyme to the garlic and cook for 1 minute more.

NUTRITION PER SERVE
Protein 32 g; Fat 61 g; Carbohydrate 65 g; Dietary Fibre 7.5 g; Cholesterol 212 mg; 3895 kJ (930 Cal)

Creamy seafood ravioli

PREPARATION TIME: 45 MINUTES + 30 MINUTES STANDING | TOTAL COOKING TIME: 20 MINUTES | SERVES 4

PASTA
250 g (9 oz/2 cups) plain (all-purpose) flour
pinch of salt
3 eggs
1 tablespoon olive oil
1 egg yolk, extra

FILLING
50 g (1¾ oz) salted butter, softened
3 garlic cloves, finely chopped
2 tablespoons finely chopped flat-leaf
   (Italian) parsley
100 g (3½ oz) scallops, cleaned and finely
   chopped
100 g (3½ oz) raw prawn meat, finely
   chopped

SAUCE
3 tablespoons salted butter
3 tablespoons plain (all-purpose) flour
375 ml (13 fl oz/1½ cups) milk
300 ml (10½ fl oz) pouring (whipping) cream
125 ml (4 fl oz/½ cup) white wine
50 g (1¾ oz/½ cup) grated parmesan cheese
2 tablespoons chopped flat-leaf (Italian)
   parsley

NUTRITION PER SERVE
Protein 30 g; Fat 40 g; Carbohydrate 57 g; Dietary
Fibre 4 g; Cholesterol 322 mg; 3035 kJ (725 Cal)

1 To make the pasta, sift the flour and salt into a bowl and make a well in the centre. Whisk the eggs, oil and 1 tablespoon water in a bowl, then add gradually to the flour and mix to a firm dough. Gather into a ball. Knead on a lightly floured surface for 5 minutes, or until smooth and elastic. Place in a lightly oiled bowl, cover with plastic wrap and set aside for 30 minutes.

2 To make the filling, mix together the butter, garlic, parsley, scallops and prawns. Set aside.

3 Roll out a quarter of the dough at a time until very thin (roughly 10 cm/4 inches wide when rolled). Place 1 teaspoon of filling at 5 cm (2 inch) intervals down one side of each strip. Whisk the extra egg yolk with 3 tablespoons water. Brush along one side of the dough and between the filling. Fold the dough over the filling. Repeat. Press the edges of the dough together firmly to seal. Cut between the mounds with a knife or a fluted pastry cutter. Cook in batches in a large saucepan of rapidly boiling salted water for 6 minutes each batch. Drain well and return to the pan to keep warm.

4 To make the sauce, melt the butter in a saucepan, add the flour and cook over low heat for 2 minutes. Remove from the heat and gradually stir in the combined milk, cream and wine. Cook over low heat until the sauce begins to thicken, stirring constantly to prevent lumps forming. Bring to the boil and simmer gently for 5 minutes. Add the parmesan cheese and parsley and toss with the ravioli.

Add the combined egg, oil and water gradually to the flour.

Place a teaspoon of filling at intervals down one side of the pasta.

Cut between each mound of filling with a sharp knife or cutter.

Tortellini with mushroom cream sauce

PREPARATION TIME: 10 MINUTES | TOTAL COOKING TIME: 20 MINUTES | SERVES 4

375 g (13 oz) tortellini
185 g (6½ oz) button mushrooms
1 small lemon
60 g (2¼ oz) salted butter
1 garlic clove, crushed
300 ml (10½ fl oz) pouring (whipping) cream
pinch of grated nutmeg
3 tablespoons grated parmesan cheese

1   Cook the pasta in a large saucepan of rapidly boiling salted water until *al dente*. Drain well and return to the pan to keep warm. Slice the whole mushrooms finely. Grate the lemon zest finely. Melt the butter in a medium-sized frying pan and cook the mushrooms over medium heat for 30 seconds.

2   Add the garlic, cream, lemon zest, nutmeg and some freshly ground black pepper. Stir over low heat for 1–2 minutes. Stir through the grated parmesan and cook gently for 3 minutes further.

3   Place the tortellini in a warm serving dish. Add the mushroom sauce and stir gently to combine. Serve immediately.

NUTRITION PER SERVE
Protein 20 g; Fat 36 g; Carbohydrate 90 g; Dietary Fibre 8 g; Cholesterol 110 mg; 3250 kJ (776 Cal)

Use a sharp knife to slice the whole mushrooms, including the stem.

Grate all the zest from the lemon on the finest side of a metal grater, avoiding the white pith.

Add the garlic, cream, lemon zest, black pepper and nutmeg to the sauce.

Spinach ravioli with tomatoes and goat's cheese

PREPARATION TIME: 15 MINUTES | TOTAL COOKING TIME: 1 HOUR | SERVES 4

4 roma (plum) tomatoes
6 garlic cloves, unpeeled and bruised
4 tablespoons extra virgin olive oil
2½ teaspoons caster (superfine) sugar
500 g (1 lb 2 oz) spinach ravioli
2 tablespoons red wine vinegar
90 g (3¼ oz) pitted kalamata olives
100 g (3½ oz) baby English spinach leaves
100 g (3½ oz) goat's cheese, crumbled

1   Preheat the oven to 190°C (375°F/Gas 5). Cut each tomato into eight wedges. Place on a large lightly greased baking tray, with the garlic cloves. Drizzle with 1 tablespoon of the olive oil, then sprinkle with 1 teaspoon of the sugar. Season with salt and pepper. Roast for 1 hour, or until softened and caramelised. Remove and keep warm.

2   Just before the tomatoes are ready, cook the pasta in a large saucepan of rapidly boiling salted water until *al dente*. Drain well and place in a large bowl. Remove the skins from the garlic.

3   To make the dressing, combine the remaining extra virgin olive oil with the vinegar, peeled roasted garlic and the remaining sugar in a screw-top jar and shake well. Pour over the pasta and toss gently. Add the olives, spinach, goat's cheese and roasted tomato and toss together. Serve immediately.

Roast the tomato wedges on a baking tray with the bruised garlic cloves.

When the garlic is roasted it will be easy to peel the skin away.

NUTRITION PER SERVE
Protein 15 g; Fat 25 g; Carbohydrate 40 g; Dietary Fibre 6 g; Cholesterol 30 mg; 1850 kJ (440 Cal)

Chicken ravioli with fresh tomato sauce

PREPARATION TIME: 40 MINUTES | TOTAL COOKING TIME: 40 MINUTES | SERVES 4

TOMATO SAUCE

1 tablespoon olive oil
1 large onion, chopped
2 garlic cloves, crushed
90 g (3¼ oz/⅓ cup) tomato paste
  (concentrated purée)
3 tablespoons dry red wine
170 ml (5½ fl oz/⅔ cup) chicken stock
2 tomatoes, chopped
1 tablespoon chopped basil

RAVIOLI

200 g (7 oz) minced (ground) chicken
1 tablespoon chopped basil
25 g (1 oz/¼ cup) grated parmesan cheese
3 spring onions (scallions), finely chopped
50 g (1¾ oz) ricotta cheese
250 g (9 oz) packet round won ton or gow
  gee wrappers

1 To make the tomato sauce, heat the oil in a saucepan and cook the onion and garlic for 2–3 minutes, then stir in the tomato paste, wine, stock and tomato and simmer for 20 minutes. Stir in the basil.

2 To make the ravioli, combine the chicken, basil, parmesan, spring onion, ricotta and some salt and pepper. Lay 24 of the won ton wrappers on a flat surface and brush with a little water. Place slightly heaped teaspoons of the mixture onto the centre of each wrapper. Place another wrapper on top and press the edges together.

3 Bring a large saucepan of salted water to the boil. Add the ravioli, a few at a time, and cook for 2–3 minutes, or until just tender. Drain well and serve with the tomato sauce.

NUTRITION PER SERVE
Protein 24 g; Fat 6 g; Carbohydrate 50 g; Dietary Fibre 6 g; Cholesterol 37 mg; 1517 kJ (363 Cal)

For the tomato sauce, add the basil to the tomato mixture.

For the ravioli, combine the chicken, basil, parmesan, spring onion and ricotta.

Place the mixture between two wrappers and press together to make the ravioli.

Cheese tortellini with capsicum and almond sauce

PREPARATION TIME: 15 MINUTES | TOTAL COOKING TIME: 15 MINUTES | SERVES 4

1 red capsicum (pepper)
1 yellow capsicum (pepper)
60 g (2¼ oz/⅔ cup) flaked almonds
8 spring onions (scallions)
2 garlic cloves, crushed
500 g (1 lb 2 oz) cheese tortellini
170 ml (5½ fl oz/⅔ cup) olive oil
30 g (1 oz/⅓ cup) finely grated pecorino
cheese

1 Cut the capsicums into large pieces, removing the seeds and membrane. Place skin side up under a hot grill (broiler) until the skin blackens and blisters. Cool under a tea towel (dish towel) or in a plastic bag, then peel away the skin. Spread the almonds on a grill tray and grill (broil) for 1–2 minutes, or until lightly toasted.

2 Roughly chop the spring onions and finely slice the green tops for garnish. Put the capsicum, almonds, spring onion and garlic in a food processor and pulse until chopped.

3 Cook the pasta in a large saucepan of rapidly boiling salted water until *al dente*. Drain well and return to the pan to keep warm. Toss the capsicum mixture through the pasta, then add the oil and cheese. Season to taste. Serve garnished with the green spring onion tops.

NUTRITION PER SERVE
Protein 24 g; Fat 64 g; Carbohydrate 36 g; Dietary Fibre 6.5 g; Cholesterol 49 mg; 3355 kJ (800 Cal)

Grill the capsicums skin side up until the skin blackens and will peel away instantly.

Put the capsicum, almonds, spring onion and garlic in a food processor to chop.

Toss the capsicum sauce through the pasta, then add the oil and cheese.

Tortellini with eggplant sauce

PREPARATION TIME: 10 MINUTES | TOTAL COOKING TIME: 20 MINUTES | SERVES 4

500 g (1 lb 2 oz) fresh tortellini
3 tablespoons olive oil
2 garlic cloves, crushed
1 red capsicum (pepper), cut into squares
500 g (1 lb 2 oz) eggplant (aubergine), cut into
    small cubes
425 g (15 oz) tinned chopped tomatoes
250 ml (9 fl oz/1 cup) vegetable stock
 2 small handfuls chopped basil

1   Cook the pasta in a large saucepan of rapidly boiling salted water until *al dente.* Drain well and return to the pan to keep warm.

2   Meanwhile, heat the oil in a large saucepan and cook the garlic and capsicum for 1 minute over medium heat. Add the eggplant and stir for 5 minutes or until lightly browned. Add the tomatoes and vegetable stock. Stir to combine and bring to the boil. Reduce the heat to low, cover and cook for 10 minutes or until the vegetables are tender. Add the basil and pasta and toss together.

HINT: *Chop the eggplant just before using as it turns brown when exposed to the air.*

Cook the tortellini in boiling water until *al dente* and then drain and return to the pan.

Add the eggplant, tomato and vegetable stock and bring to the boil.

NUTRITION PER SERVE
Protein 17 g; Fat 17 g; Carbohydrate 96 g; Dietary Fibre 11 g; Cholesterol 0 mg; 2559 kJ (611 Cal)

Baked pasta

Classic lasagne

PREPARATION TIME: 25 MINUTES | TOTAL COOKING TIME: 1 HOUR 15 MINUTES | SERVES 4–6

250 g (9 oz) lasagne sheets
75 g (2½ oz/½ cup) grated mozzarella cheese
60 g (2¼ oz/½ cup) grated cheddar cheese
125 ml (4 fl oz/½ cup) pouring (whipping) cream
3 tablespoons grated parmesan cheese

CHEESE SAUCE
60 g (2¼ oz) salted butter
40 g (1½ oz/⅓ cup) plain (all-purpose) flour
500 ml (17 fl oz/2 cups) milk
125 g (4½ oz/1 cup) grated cheddar cheese

MEAT SAUCE
1 tablespoon olive oil
1 onion, finely chopped
1 garlic clove, crushed
500 g (1 lb 2 oz) minced (ground) beef
850 g (1 lb 14 oz) tinned chopped tomatoes
3 tablespoons dry red wine
½ teaspoon ground oregano
¼ teaspoon ground basil

NUTRITION PER SERVE (6)
Protein 41 g; Fat 58 g; Carbohydrate 45 g; Dietary
Fibre 5 g; Cholesterol 170 mg; 3765 kJ (899 Cal)

1 Preheat the oven to 180°C (350°F/Gas 4). Brush a shallow ovenproof dish approximately 24 x 30 cm (9½ x 12 inches) with melted butter or oil. Line with lasagne sheets, breaking them to fill any gaps, and set aside.

2 To make the cheese sauce, melt the butter in a saucepan. Add the flour and stir for 1 minute. Remove from the heat and slowly add the milk, stirring until smooth. Return to the heat and cook, stirring, over medium heat until the sauce boils and thickens. Reduce the heat and simmer for 3 minutes. Stir in the cheese, season and set aside.

3 To make the meat sauce, heat the oil in a large saucepan. Add the onion and garlic and stir over low heat until the onion is tender. Add the minced beef and brown well, breaking up with a wooden spoon as it cooks. Stir in the tomato, wine, oregano, basil and season. Bring to the boil, reduce the heat and simmer for 20 minutes.

4 Spoon one-third of the meat sauce over the lasagne sheets. Top with one-third of the cheese sauce. Arrange another layer of lasagne sheets over the top.

5 Continue layering, finishing with lasagne sheets. Sprinkle with the combined mozzarella and cheddar cheeses. Pour the cream over the top. Sprinkle with parmesan cheese. Bake for 35–40 minutes, or until golden.

Arrange a layer of lasagne sheets in the base of an ovenproof dish.

Spread a layer of meat sauce over the lasagne sheets and then build up the layers.

Speedy chicken and pasta bake

PREPARATION TIME: 15 MINUTES | TOTAL COOKING TIME: 45 MINUTES | SERVES 4

200 g (7 oz) spiral pasta
425 g (15 oz) tinned cream of mushroom or
　　broccoli soup
250 g (9 oz/1 cup) sour cream
1 teaspoon curry powder
1 barbecued chicken
250 g (9 oz) broccoli, cut into florets
90 g (3¼ oz/1 cup) fresh breadcrumbs
185 g (6½ oz/1½ cups) grated cheddar cheese

1　Preheat the oven to 180°C (350°F/Gas 4).
Cook the pasta in a large saucepan of rapidly
boiling salted water until *al dente*. Drain well
and return to the pan to keep warm.

2　Combine the soup, sour cream and curry
powder and season to taste with freshly ground
black pepper.

3　Remove the meat from the chicken and
roughly chop. Combine the chicken with
the pasta, broccoli and soup mixture. Spoon
into four lightly greased 500 ml (17 fl oz/
2 cup) ovenproof dishes and sprinkle with the
combined breadcrumbs and cheese. Bake for
25–30 minutes, or until the cheese melts.

VARIATION: *This recipe can be made in a 2 litre*
(70 fl oz/8 cup) ovenproof dish and baked for
40 minutes, or until the cheese has melted.

Mix together the soup, sour cream and curry
powder to make the sauce.

Mix together the chicken meat, pasta, broccoli
and sauce.

NUTRITION PER SERVE
Protein 67 g; Fat 47 g; Carbohydrate 55 g; Dietary
Fibre 8 g; Cholesterol 254 mg; 3812 kJ (911 Cal)

Macaroni cheese

PREPARATION TIME: 15 MINUTES | TOTAL COOKING TIME: 35 MINUTES | SERVES 4

225 g (8 oz) macaroni
90 g (3¼ oz) salted butter
1 onion, finely chopped
3 tablespoons plain (all-purpose) flour
500 ml (17 fl oz/2 cups) milk
2 teaspoons wholegrain mustard
150 g (5½ oz) mature cheddar cheese, grated
100 g (3½ oz) cheddar cheese, grated
30 g (1 oz) fresh breadcrumbs

1 Cook the pasta in a large saucepan of rapidly boiling salted water until *al dente*. Drain well and return to the pan to keep warm.

2 Preheat the oven to 180°C (350°F/Gas 4). Grease a 1.5 litre (52 fl oz/6 cup) ovenproof dish.

3 Melt the butter in a large saucepan over low heat, add the onion and cook for 5 minutes, or until softened. Stir in the flour and cook for 1 minute, or until pale and foaming. Remove from the heat and gradually stir in the milk. Return to the heat and stir constantly until the sauce boils and thickens. Reduce the heat and simmer for 2 minutes. Stir in the mustard and about three-quarters of the combined cheeses. Season to taste. Add the cooked pasta to the pan and stir until coated in the mixture. Spoon into the dish and smooth the surface.

4 Combine the breadcrumbs and remaining cheese and scatter over the top. Bake for about 15 minutes, or until golden brown and bubbling.

NUTRITION PER SERVE
Protein 30 g; Fat 45 g; Carbohydrate 60 g; Dietary Fibre 4 g; Cholesterol 130 mg; 3087 kJ (737 Cal)

Salmon and ricotta-stuffed conchiglione

PREPARATION TIME: 15 MINUTES | TOTAL COOKING TIME: 50 MINUTES | SERVES 4

200 g (7 oz) conchiglione (large pasta shells)

425 g (15 oz) tinned red salmon, drained, bones removed, flaked

500 g (1 lb 2 oz/2 cups) ricotta cheese

1 tablespoon chopped flat-leaf (Italian) parsley

3 tablespoons snipped chives

1½ celery stalks, finely chopped

90 g (3¼ oz/¾ cup) grated cheddar cheese

185 ml (6 fl oz/¾ cup) pouring (whipping) cream

30 g (1 oz) grated parmesan cheese

1 Preheat the oven to 180°C (350°F/Gas 4). Cook the pasta in a large saucepan of rapidly boiling salted water until *al dente*. Drain well and return to the pan to keep warm.

2 Combine the salmon, ricotta, parsley, chives, celery and cheddar cheese in a bowl and season to taste with salt and freshly ground black pepper.

3 Place 2 teaspoons of filling in each shell. Arrange in a single layer in a 3 litre (105 fl oz/12 cup) ovenproof dish. Pour on the cream and sprinkle with parmesan. Cover with foil and bake for 20 minutes, then remove the foil and return to the oven for 15 minutes, or until golden brown. Serve with the sauce spooned over the shells.

NUTRITION PER SERVE
Protein 31 g; Fat 36 g; Carbohydrate 38 g; Dietary Fibre 3 g; Cholesterol 135 mg; 2470 kJ (590 Cal)

Cook the large pasta shells until they are tender, then drain.

Mix together the salmon, ricotta, parsley, chives, celery and cheddar cheese.

Arrange the shells in a single layer in an ovenproof dish, then top with cream and parmesan.

Orzo and Greek cheese bake

PREPARATION TIME: 15 MINUTES | TOTAL COOKING TIME: 40 MINUTES | SERVES 6

415 g (14¾ oz/2 cups) orzo
60 g (2¼ oz) salted butter
6 spring onions (scallions), chopped
450 g (1 lb) English spinach, chopped
2 tablespoons plain (all-purpose) flour
1.25 litres (44 fl oz/5 cups) milk
250 g (9 oz) kefalotyri cheese, grated
  (see NOTE)
250 g (9 oz) marinated feta cheese, drained
3 tablespoons chopped dill

1 Preheat the oven to 190°C (375°F/Gas 5). Cook the pasta in a large saucepan of rapidly boiling salted water until *al dente*. Drain well and return to the pan keep warm. Heat 1 tablespoon of the butter in a large saucepan over high heat and cook the spring onion for 30 seconds. Add the spinach and stir for 1 minute, or until wilted. Season and stir into the pasta.

2 Put the remaining butter in the saucepan in which the spinach was cooked. Melt over low heat, then stir in the flour and cook for 1 minute, or until pale and foaming. Remove from the heat and gradually stir in the milk. Return to the heat and stir constantly for 5 minutes, or until the sauce boils and thickens. Add two-thirds of the kefalotyri and all of the feta and stir for 2 minutes until melted. Remove from the heat and stir in the dill.

3 Combine the pasta mixture with the cheese sauce, season to taste and pour into a lightly greased 2.5 litre (87 fl oz/10 cup) ovenproof dish. Sprinkle the remaining cheese on top and bake for 15 minutes, or until golden.

NOTE: *Kefalotyri is a hard Greek sheep's milk cheese; it is similar to parmesan.*

Cook the spinach until wilted, then season well and stir into the orzo.

Mix together the pasta and spinach with the cheese sauce.

NUTRITION PER SERVE
Protein 31 g; Fat 34 g; Carbohydrate 63 g; Dietary Fibre 6 g; Cholesterol 103 mg; 2835 kJ (680 Cal)

Chicken, broccoli and pasta bake

PREPARATION TIME: 15 MINUTES | TOTAL COOKING TIME: 35 MINUTES | SERVES 6–8

300 g (10½ oz) pasta
425 g (15 oz) tinned cream of mushroom soup
2 eggs
185 g (6½ oz/¾ cup) mayonnaise
1 tablespoon dijon mustard
200 g (7 oz) grated cheddar cheese
600 g (1 lb 5 oz) boneless, skinless chicken
    breasts, thinly sliced
400 g (14 oz) frozen broccoli pieces, thawed
40 g (1½ oz/½ cup) fresh breadcrumbs

1 Preheat the oven to 180°C (350°F/Gas 4).
Cook the pasta in a large saucepan of rapidly
boiling salted water until *al dente*. Drain well
and return to the pan to keep warm. Combine
the soup, eggs, mayonnaise, mustard and half the
cheese in a bowl.

2 Heat a lightly greased non-stick frying pan
over medium heat, add the chicken and cook for
5–6 minutes, or until cooked through. Season
with salt and pepper, then set aside to cool.

3 Add the chicken and broccoli to the pasta.
Pour the soup mixture over the top and stir.
Transfer the mixture to a 3 litre ovenproof dish.
Sprinkle with combined breadcrumbs and
remaining cheese. Bake for 20 minutes, or until it
becomes golden brown.

NUTRITION PER SERVE (8)
Protein 34 g; Fat 33 g; Carbohydrate 33 g; Dietary
Fibre 4.5 g; Cholesterol 143 mg; 2340 kJ (560 Cal)

Mix together the soup, eggs, mayonnaise, mustard and half the cheese.

Cook the chicken in a lightly greased non-stick frying pan.

Mix together the chicken, broccoli and soup mixture and then put it in the dish.

Beef and spinach cannelloni

PREPARATION TIME: 35 MINUTES | TOTAL COOKING TIME: 1 HOUR 10 MINUTES | SERVES 4–6

FILLING
1 tablespoon olive oil
1 onion, chopped
1 garlic clove, crushed
500 g (1 lb 2 oz) minced (ground) beef
250 g (9 oz) frozen spinach, thawed
3 tablespoons tomato paste
    (concentrated purée)
125 g (4½ oz/½ cup) ricotta cheese
1 egg
½ teaspoon ground oregano

BECHAMEL SAUCE
250 ml (9 fl oz/1 cup) milk
1 parsley sprig
5 peppercorns
30 g (1 oz) salted butter
1 tablespoon plain (all-purpose) flour
125 ml (4 fl oz/½ cup) pouring (whipping)
    cream

TOMATO SAUCE
425 g (15 oz) tin tomato passata
    (puréed tomato)
2 tablespoons chopped basil
1 garlic clove, crushed
½ teaspoon sugar

12–15 instant cannelloni tubes
150 g (5½ oz/1 cup) grated mozzarella cheese
60 g (2¼ oz/½ cup) grated parmesan cheese

1 Preheat the oven to 180°C (350°F/Gas 4). To make the filling, heat the oil in a frying pan. Add the onion and garlic; stir over low heat until onion is tender. Add the beef and brown well. Add spinach and tomato paste. Cook, stirring, for 1 minute. Remove from the heat. Mix the ricotta, egg and oregano. Stir into the beef mixture.

2 To make the béchamel sauce, put the milk, parsley and peppercorns in a small saucepan. Bring to the boil. Remove from heat and cool for 10 minutes. Strain, discarding the flavourings. Melt the butter in a small saucepan and stir in the flour. Cook, stirring, for 1 minute. Remove from the heat. Gradually stir in the strained milk until smooth. Return to the heat and stir constantly over medium heat until the sauce boils and thickens. Reduce heat and simmer for 3 minutes. Add cream and season.

3 To make the tomato sauce, put all the ingredients in a pan and bring to the boil. Reduce the heat and simmer for 5 minutes. Pipe the filling into cannelloni tubes. Spoon a little of the tomato sauce in the base of a large ovenproof dish. Arrange the cannelloni on top. Pour béchamel sauce over the cannelloni, followed by the remaining tomato sauce. Sprinkle the cheeses over the top. Bake for 30–35 minutes, or until golden.

NUTRITION PER SERVE (6)
Protein 40 g; Fat 30 g; Carbohydrate 68 g; Dietary Fibre 9 g; Cholesterol 120 mg; 3010 kJ (720 Cal)

Add the milk slowly to the béchamel sauce, stirring constantly to prevent lumps.

You can use a piping bag to fill the cannelloni, but if you don't have one a teaspoon will do.

Spoon tomato sauce into the dish and then top with a layer of cannelloni.

Baked spaghetti frittata

PREPARATION TIME: 15 MINUTES | TOTAL COOKING TIME: 35 MINUTES | SERVES 4

30 g (1 oz) salted butter
125 g (4½ oz) button mushrooms, sliced
1 red or green capsicum (pepper), seeded and
    chopped
125 g (4½ oz) ham, sliced
90 g (3¼ oz/½ cup) frozen peas
6 eggs
250 ml (9 fl oz/1 cup) pouring (whipping)
    cream or milk
100 g (3½ oz) cooked spaghetti, chopped
2 tablespoons chopped parsley
3 tablespoons grated parmesan cheese

1 Preheat the oven to 180°C (350°F/ Gas 4). Grease a 23 cm (9 inch) round ovenproof dish. Melt the butter in a frying pan and add the mushrooms. Cook over low heat for 2–3 minutes.

2 Add the capsicum and cook for 1 minute. Stir in the ham and peas. Remove from the heat to cool slightly.

3 Whisk together the eggs and cream and season. Add the spaghetti, parsley and mushroom mixture and stir. Pour into the dish and sprinkle with parmesan cheese. Bake for 25–30 minutes.

NUTRITION PER SERVE
Protein 23 g; Fat 38 g; Carbohydrate 23 g; Dietary Fibre 4 g; Cholesterol 110 mg; 2170 kJ (518 Cal)

Cook the mushrooms in the butter over low heat for 2–3 minutes.

Stir in the ham and frozen peas and then remove from the heat to cool slightly.

Whisk together the eggs, cream, and some salt and pepper.

Baked seafood pasta

PREPARATION TIME: 15 MINUTES | TOTAL COOKING TIME: 45 MINUTES | SERVES 4–6

250 g (9 oz) lasagne sheets

500 g (1 lb 2 oz) boneless fish fillets

125 g (4½ oz) scallops

500 g (1 lb 2 oz) raw prawns (shrimp), peeled and deveined

125 g (4½ oz) salted butter

1 leek, sliced

90 g (3¼ oz/¾ cup) plain (all-purpose) flour

500 ml (17 fl oz/2 cups) milk

500 ml (17 fl oz/2 cups) dry white wine

125 g (4½ oz/1 cup) grated cheddar cheese

125 ml (4 fl oz/½ cup) pouring (whipping) cream

60 g (2¼ oz) grated parmesan cheese

2 tablespoons chopped parsley

1 Preheat the oven to 180°C (350°F/ Gas 4). Grease a shallow 24 x 30 cm (9½ x 12 inch) ovenproof dish and line with lasagne sheets, breaking them to fill any gaps. Chop the fish and scallops into bite-sized pieces. Chop the prawns.

2 Melt the butter in a large saucepan and cook the leek, stirring, for 1 minute. Add the flour and cook, stirring, for 1 minute. Remove from the heat and slowly stir in the milk and wine until smooth. Return to medium heat and stir constantly until the sauce boils and thickens. Reduce the heat and simmer for 3 minutes. Stir in the cheddar cheese and seafood, season and simmer for 1 minute.

3 Spoon half the seafood sauce over the lasagne sheets. Top with another layer of lasagne sheets. Continue layering the sauce and the sheets, finishing with lasagne sheets.

4 Pour the cream over the top. Sprinkle with the combined parmesan and parsley and bake for 30 minutes, or until bubbling and golden.

NUTRITION PER SERVE (6)
Protein 57 g; Fat 28 g; Carbohydrate 45 g; Dietary Fibre 3 g; Cholesterol 264 mg; 3000 kJ (720 Cal)

Cut the fish and scallops into bite-sized pieces and chop the prawns.

Slowly stir in the wine and milk and stir until the sauce is smooth.

Ricotta, eggplant and pasta timbales

PREPARATION TIME: 15 MINUTES | TOTAL COOKING TIME: 45 MINUTES | MAKES 4

125 ml (4 fl oz/½ cup) light olive oil
1 large eggplant (aubergine), cut lengthways
    into thin slices
200 g (7 oz) macaroni
1 small onion, finely chopped
2 garlic cloves, crushed
400 g (14 oz) tinned chopped tomatoes
400 g (14 oz) ricotta cheese
90 g (3¼ oz) roughly grated parmesan cheese
1 handful shredded basil

NUTRITION PER TIMBALE
Protein 26 g; Fat 40 g; Carbohydrate 43 g; Dietary
Fibre 6 g; Cholesterol 67 mg; 2645 kJ (630 Cal)

1   Preheat the oven to 180°C (350°F/Gas 4). Heat 2 tablespoons of the oil in a large, non-stick frying pan and cook the eggplant in three batches over medium heat for 2–3 minutes on each side, or until golden, adding 2 tablespoons of the oil with each batch. Remove from the pan and drain on crumpled paper towels. Meanwhile, cook the pasta in a large saucepan of rapidly boiling salted water until *al dente*. Drain well and return to the pan to keep warm.

2   Add the onion and garlic to the frying pan and cook over medium heat for 2–3 minutes, or until just golden. Add the tomato and cook for 5 minutes, or until the sauce is pulpy and most of the liquid has evaporated. Season, then remove from the heat.

3   Combine the ricotta, parmesan cheese and basil in a large bowl, then mix in the pasta. Line four 375 ml (13 fl oz/1½ cup) ramekins with eggplant, trimming to fit the base and sides. Top with half the pasta mix, pressing down firmly. Spoon on the tomato sauce, then cover with the remaining pasta mix. Bake for 10–15 minutes, or until heated through and golden on top. Leave for 5 minutes, then run a knife around the ramekins to loosen the timbales before turning out.

Cut the eggplant lengthways into slices and then fry in batches.

Add the tomato to the sauce and cook until pulpy and the liquid has evaporated.

Line the ramekins with eggplant then fill with pasta and tomato sauce.

Pasta pie

PREPARATION TIME: 15 MINUTES | TOTAL COOKING TIME: 55 MINUTES | SERVES 4

250 g (9 oz) macaroni
1 tablespoon olive oil
1 onion, sliced
125 g (4½ oz) pancetta, chopped
125 g (4½ oz) ham, chopped
4 eggs
250 ml (9 fl oz/1 cup) milk
250 ml (9 fl oz/1 cup) pouring (whipping)
    cream
2 tablespoons snipped chives
120 g (4¼ oz) grated cheddar cheese
125 g (4½ oz) bocconcini (fresh baby
    mozzarella cheese), chopped

1   Preheat the oven to 180°C (350°F/Gas 4). Cook the pasta in a large saucepan of rapidly boiling salted water until *al dente*. Drain well. Spread evenly over the base of a greased deep ovenproof dish.

2   Heat the oil in a large frying pan and cook the onion over low heat until tender. Add the pancetta and cook for 2 minutes. Add the ham and stir well. Remove from the heat to cool.

3   Whisk together the eggs, milk, cream, chives and season. Add the cheddar cheese, chopped bocconcini and the pancetta mixture and stir well. Spread evenly over the macaroni. Bake for 35–40 minutes, or until set.

HINT: *Serve with slices of roma (plum) tomato.*

Cook the pasta and drain well, then spread in the ovenproof dish.

Add the cheddar, chopped bocconcini and the pancetta mixture.

NUTRITION PER SERVE
Protein 50 g; Fat 70 g; Carbohydrate 50 g; Dietary Fibre 4 g; Cholesterol 386 mg; 4300 kJ (1027 Cal)

Baked shells with ricotta and prosciutto

PREPARATION TIME: 15 MINUTES | TOTAL COOKING TIME: 45 MINUTES | SERVES 4–6

24 conchiglione (large pasta shells)

200 g (7 oz) prosciutto, roughly chopped

2 tablespoons snipped chives

2 very large handfuls chopped basil

90 g (3¼ oz) salted butter

500 g (1 lb 2 oz/2 cup) ricotta cheese

150 g (5½ oz/1 cup) chopped sun-dried
    capsicum

100 g (3½ oz/1 cup) grated parmesan cheese

750 ml (26 fl oz/3 cups) bottled tomato pasta
    sauce

1 Preheat the oven to 180°C (350°F/Gas 4). Cook the pasta in a large saucepan of rapidly boiling salted water until *al dente*. Drain well and return to the pan to keep warm. Place the prosciutto, chives and basil in a food processor or blender and pulse until chopped.

2 Melt the butter in a large frying pan over medium heat. Add the prosciutto mixture and cook for about 5 minutes, or until the prosciutto is golden and crisp. Transfer the mixture to a bowl, add the ricotta cheese, capsicum and a quarter of the parmesan cheese. Stir well and season to taste.

3 Pour the pasta sauce into a 3 litre (105 fl oz/12 cup) ovenproof dish. Spoon the ricotta mixture into the pasta shells and place in the dish. Sprinkle the remaining parmesan cheese over the shells and bake for 25–30 minutes, or until golden. Spoon the sauce over the shells and serve.

Finely chop the prosciutto, chives and basil in a food processor.

Spoon the filling into the pasta shells and then arrange them in the dish.

NUTRITION PER SERVE (6)
Protein 27 g; Fat 28 g; Carbohydrate 32 g; Dietary Fibre 4.5 g; Cholesterol 107 mg; 2040 kJ (485 Cal)

Seafood cannelloni

PREPARATION TIME: 30 MINUTES | TOTAL COOKING TIME: 1 HOUR 55 MINUTES | SERVES 6

1 onion, sliced
1 carrot, sliced
1 celery stalk, cut in half
1 bouquet garni
250 ml (9 fl oz/1 cup) dry white wine
4 whole black peppercorns
300 g (10½ oz) scallops
500 g (1 lb 2 oz) raw prawns (shrimp), peeled
    and deveined
300 g (10½ oz) skinless fish fillets
    (such as flathead, flake, hake, ling, cod),
    boned and chopped
60 g (2¼ oz) salted butter
1 onion, finely chopped
200 g (7 oz) button mushrooms, finely
    chopped
800 g (1 lb 12 oz) tinned chopped tomatoes
2 tablespoons chopped parsley
2 tablespoons chopped basil
2 tablespoons pouring (whipping) cream
15 cannelloni tubes
125 g (4½ oz) grated cheddar cheese

BECHAMEL SAUCE
60 g (2¼ oz) salted butter
2 tablespoons plain (all-purpose) flour
750 ml (26 fl oz/3 cups) milk

NUTRITION PER SERVE
Protein 56 g; Fat 35 g; Carbohydrate 76 g; Dietary
Fibre 8 g; Cholesterol 274 mg; 3638 kJ (869 Cal)

1 Preheat the oven to 180°C (350°F/Gas 4). Combine the onion, carrot, celery, bouquet garni and 500 ml (17 fl oz/2 cups) water in a large saucepan and bring to the boil. Reduce the heat and simmer for 15 minutes. Add the wine and peppercorns and simmer for 15 minutes. Strain, discard the vegetables and reserve the liquid.

2 Cut the seafood small enough to fit in the cannelloni tubes.

3 Put the reserved liquid in a clean saucepan. Bring to the boil. Add the seafood. Reduce the heat and simmer until tender. Strain and reserve the liquid.

4 Melt the butter in a large frying pan, add the onion and cook until golden brown. Add the mushrooms and cook until tender. Add 3 tablespoons of the reserved liquid, tomato and herbs; bring to the boil. Reduce the heat; simmer for 30 minutes, or until the sauce thickens. Stir in the seafood and cream. Season.

5 To make the sauce, melt butter in a saucepan, add flour; stir for 1 minute, or until pale and foaming. Remove from the heat and gradually stir in milk. Return to heat and stir until the sauce comes to the boil and thickens.

6 Spoon the mixture into the cannelloni tubes. Place in a greased 3 litre (105 fl oz/12 cup) ovenproof dish. Pour the sauce over and sprinkle with grated cheese. Bake for 40 minutes, or until cannelloni tubes are tender.

Cut all the seafood into pieces small enough to fit in the cannelloni tubes.

Drain the seafood through a strainer reserving the poaching liquid.

Use a teaspoon or piping bag to insert the seafood mixture into the cannelloni tubes.

Pasta and spinach timbales

PREPARATION TIME: 15 MINUTES | TOTAL COOKING TIME: 40 MINUTES | SERVES 6

30 g (1 oz) salted butter
1 tablespoon olive oil
1 onion, chopped
500 g (1 lb 2 oz) English spinach, blanched
8 eggs, beaten
250 ml (9 fl oz/1 cup) pouring (whipping) cream
100 g (3½ oz) spaghetti, cooked
60 g (2¼ oz/½ cup) grated cheddar cheese
60 g (2¼ oz/½ cup) grated parmesan cheese

1   Preheat the oven to 180°C (350°F/Gas 4). Brush six 250 ml (9 fl oz/1 cup) ramekins with melted butter or oil. Line the bases with baking paper. Heat the butter and oil together in a frying pan. Add the onion and stir over low heat until tender. Add the well-drained spinach and cook for 1 minute. Remove from the heat and allow to cool. Whisk in the eggs and cream. Stir in the spaghetti, grated cheeses and season; stir well. Spoon into the ramekins.

2   Place the ramekins in a roasting tin. Pour boiling water into the tin to come halfway up the sides of the ramekins. Bake for 30–35 minutes, or until set. Halfway through cooking, you may need to cover with a sheet of foil to prevent overbrowning. Near the end of cooking time, test the timbales with the point of a knife—the knife should come out clean.

3   Allow the timbales to rest for 15 minutes, then run the point of a knife around the edge of each ramekin and turn out onto serving plates.

Let the mixture cool for a while before you add the eggs and cream.

Leave the timbales to rest for 15 minutes then run the tip of a knife around the edge of each one.

NUTRITION PER SERVE
Protein 16 g; Fat 20 g; Carbohydrate 13 g; Dietary Fibre 2 g; Cholesterol 260 mg; 1280 kJ (300 Cal)

Pasta-filled capsicums

PREPARATION TIME: 20 MINUTES | TOTAL COOKING TIME: 45 MINUTES | SERVES 4–6

1 tablespoon olive oil

1 onion, finely chopped

1 garlic clove, crushed

3 bacon slices, finely chopped

150 g (5½ oz) risoni, cooked

150 g (5½ oz/1 cup) grated mozzarella cheese

60 g (2¼ oz/½ cup) grated parmesan cheese

2 tablespoons chopped parsley

4 large red capsicums (peppers), halved
lengthways, seeds removed

425 g (15 oz) tinned chopped tomatoes

125 ml (4 fl oz/½ cup) dry white wine

1 tablespoon tomato paste (concentrated
purée)

½ teaspoon ground oregano

2 tablespoons chopped basil

1 Preheat the oven to 180°C (350°F/Gas 4). Lightly grease a large shallow ovenproof dish. Heat the oil in a frying pan and cook the onion and garlic over low heat until tender. Add the bacon and stir until crisp.

2 Transfer to a large bowl and add the risoni, cheeses and parsley. Spoon into the capsicum halves and arrange in the dish.

3 Combine the tomato, wine, tomato paste and oregano. Season well, then spoon over the risoni mixture. Sprinkle with basil. Bake for about 35–40 minutes.

Cook the onion and garlic until tender, then add the bacon and cook until crisp.

Spoon the risoni and cheese mixture into the capsicum halves.

Baked macaroni with butter sauce

PREPARATION TIME: 15 MINUTES + 5 MINUTES RESTING | TOTAL COOKING TIME: 40 MINUTES | SERVES 4

200 g (7 oz) macaroni

150 g (5½ oz) salted butter

30 g (1 oz/¼ cup) plain (all-purpose) flour

600 ml (21 fl oz) milk

1 egg, lightly beaten

185 g (6½ oz/1½ cups) grated cheddar
cheese

2 garlic cloves, crushed

2 ripe tomatoes, seeded and diced

1 Preheat the oven to 180°C (350°F/ Gas 4). Lightly grease four shallow 250 ml (9 fl oz/1 cup) ramekins. Cook the pasta in a large saucepan of rapidly boiling salted water until *al dente*. Drain well and return to the pan to keep warm. Meanwhile, melt 60 g (2¼ oz) of the butter in a large saucepan, add the flour and cook, stirring, over low heat for 1 minute. Remove from the heat and gradually add the milk, stirring until smooth. Return to the heat and cook, stirring, over medium heat for 4 minutes, or until the mixture boils and thickens. Reduce the heat and simmer for 1 minute. Remove from the heat and season well.

2 Add the pasta, egg and two-thirds of the cheese and stir until well combined. Spoon into the dishes and sprinkle with the remaining cheese. Place the ramekins in a roasting tin and pour enough boiling water into the tin to come halfway up the side. Bake for 25 minutes, or until set. Remove from the roasting tin and leave to rest for 5 minutes.

3 To make the sauce, melt the remaining butter in a frying pan. Add the garlic and tomato and stir over medium heat for 2 minutes. Turn out the baked macaroni onto plates and spoon the warm sauce around the outside. Serve immediately.

NUTRITION PER SERVE
Protein 26 g; Fat 57 g; Carbohydrate 50 g; Dietary Fibre 4 g; Cholesterol 215 mg; 3385 kJ (810 Cal)

Add the milk to the sauce slowly, stirring until smooth before returning to the heat.

Spoon the pasta, egg and cheese into the ramekins and sprinkle with the remaining cheese.

Melt the butter in a frying pan and add the garlic and tomato.

Baked fettuccine

PREPARATION TIME: 20 MINUTES I TOTAL COOKING TIME: 25 MINUTES I SERVES 4–6

500 g (1 lb 2 oz) spinach fettuccine
60 g (2¼ oz) salted butter
1 onion, finely chopped
300 g (10½ oz) sour cream
250 ml (9 fl oz/1 cup) pouring (whipping) cream
¼ teaspoon ground nutmeg
60 g (2¼ oz) grated parmesan cheese
150 g (5½ oz/1 cup) grated mozzarella cheese

1   Preheat the oven to 180°C (350°F/Gas 4). Cook the pasta in a large saucepan of rapidly boiling salted water until *al dente*. Drain well.

2   Meanwhile, melt the butter in a large saucepan and cook the onion over low heat until tender. Add the pasta. Add the sour cream and toss well. Simmer, stirring, until the pasta is well coated.

3   Stir in the cream, nutmeg and half the parmesan cheese and season well. Pour into a greased ovenproof dish. Sprinkle with the combined mozzarella and remaining parmesan. Bake for 15 minutes, or until golden.

NUTRITION PER SERVE (6)
Protein 30 g; Fat 55 g; Carbohydrate 92 g; Dietary Fibre 7 g; Cholesterol 133 mg; 4120 kJ (990 Cal)

Melt the butter in a pan and cook the onion over low heat until tender.

Add the fettuccine and sour cream to the pan and simmer until well coated.

Put the pasta in a greased dish and sprinkle with mozzarella and parmesan.

Beef vermicelli cake

PREPARATION TIME: 10 MINUTES + 10 MINUTES STANDING | TOTAL COOKING TIME: 50 MINUTES | SERVES 4–6

90 g (3¼ oz) salted butter

1 onion, chopped

500 g (1 lb 2 oz) minced (ground) beef

800 ml (28 fl oz) bottled tomato pasta sauce

2 tablespoons tomato paste (concentrated
    purée)

250 g (9 oz) vermicelli

30 g (1 oz/¼ cup) plain (all-purpose) flour

310 ml (10¾ fl oz/1¼ cups) milk

150 g (5½ oz/1¼ cups) grated cheddar cheese

1   Preheat the oven to 180°C (350°F/Gas 4).
Lightly grease a 24 cm (9½ inch) round deep
spring-form cake tin. Melt a tablespoon of the
butter in a large deep frying pan and cook the
onion over medium heat for 2–3 minutes, or
until soft. Add the beef, breaking up any
lumps with the back of a spoon, and cook for
4–5 minutes, or until browned. Stir in the
pasta sauce and tomato paste, reduce the heat
and simmer for 20–25 minutes. Season well.

2   Cook the pasta in a large saucepan of rapidly
boiling salted water until *al dente*. Drain well.
Meanwhile, melt the remaining butter in a
saucepan over low heat. Stir in the flour and
cook for 1 minute, or until pale and foaming.
Remove from the heat and gradually stir in the
milk. Return to the heat and stir constantly until
the sauce boils and thickens. Reduce the heat
and simmer for 2 minutes.

3   Spread half the pasta over the base of the
tin, then cover with half the meat sauce. Cover
with the remaining pasta, pressing down with the
palm of your hand. Spoon on the remaining meat
sauce and then pour on the white sauce. Sprinkle
with the cheese and cook for 15 minutes. Leave
to stand for 10 minutes before removing from
the tin. Cut into wedges to serve.

Cook the beef until browned, breaking up any
lumps with a spoon.

Spread half the pasta into the tin and then cover
with half the meat sauce.

NUTRITION PER SERVE (6)
Protein 34 g; Fat 32 g; Carbohydrate 47 g; Dietary
Fibre 6 g; Cholesterol 121 mg; 2535 kJ (605 Cal)

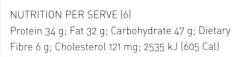

Ricotta-stuffed pasta shells with chicken sauce

PREPARATION TIME: 30 MINUTES | TOTAL COOKING TIME: 1 HOUR 10 MINUTES | SERVES 4

500 g (1 lb 2 oz) conchiglie (large pasta shells)
2 tablespoons olive oil
1 onion, chopped
1 garlic clove, crushed
60 g (2¼ oz) prosciutto, sliced
125 g (4½ oz) button mushrooms, chopped
250 g (9 oz) minced (ground) chicken
2 tablespoons tomato paste (concentrated purée)
425 g (15 oz) tin chopped tomatoes
125 ml (4 fl oz/½ cup) dry white wine
1 teaspoon dried oregano
250 g (9 oz/1 cup) ricotta cheese
220 g (7¾ oz) mozzarella cheese, grated
1 teaspoon snipped chives
1 tablespoon chopped parsley
3 tablespoons grated parmesan cheese

1   Cook the pasta in a large saucepan of rapidly boiling salted water until *al dente*. Drain well and return to the pan to keep warm.

2   Meanwhile, heat the oil in a large frying pan. Add the onion and garlic, then stir over low heat until the onion is tender. Add the prosciutto and stir for 1 minute. Add the mushrooms and cook for 2 minutes. Add the chicken and brown well, breaking up any lumps with a fork as it cooks.

3   Stir in the tomato paste, tomato, wine and oregano and season to taste. Bring to the boil, reduce the heat and simmer for 20 minutes.

4   Preheat the oven to 180°C (350°F/ Gas 4). Combine the ricotta, mozzarella, chives, parsley and half the parmesan cheese. Spoon a little into each shell. Spoon some of the chicken sauce into the base of an ovenproof dish. Arrange the conchiglie on top. Spread the remaining sauce over the top and sprinkle with the remaining parmesan. Bake 25–30 minutes, or until golden.

NUTRITION PER SERVE
Protein 43 g; Fat 23 g; Carbohydrate 95 g; Dietary Fibre 9 g; Cholesterol 76 mg; 3282 kJ (785 Cal)

Add the sliced prosciutto to the onion and garlic in a large frying pan.

Add the minced chicken and brown well, breaking it up with a fork as it cooks.

Carefully spoon some filling into each of the shells and then arrange in the dish.

Quick mushroom and ricotta cannelloni

PREPARATION TIME: 15 MINUTES | TOTAL COOKING TIME: 30 MINUTES | SERVES 4

500 g (1 lb 2 oz) button mushrooms
200 g (7 oz) fresh lasagne sheets
2 tablespoons olive oil
3 garlic cloves, crushed
2 tablespoons lemon juice
400 g (14 oz) ricotta cheese
3 tablespoons chopped basil
425 ml (15 fl oz) bottled tomato pasta sauce
150 g (5½ oz/1 cup) grated mozzarella cheese

1 Preheat the oven to 180°C (350°F/Gas 4). Finely chop the mushrooms in a food processor. Cut the lasagne sheets into twelve 13 x 16 cm (5 x 6¼ inch) rectangles.

2 Heat the oil in a large frying pan over medium heat. Add the garlic and mushrooms and cook, stirring, for 3 minutes. Add the lemon juice and cook for a further 2 minutes, or until the mushrooms are softened. Transfer to a sieve over a bowl to collect the juices, pressing with a spoon to remove as much moisture as possible. Reserve.

3 Place the mushrooms in a bowl with the ricotta and basil. Season generously and mix well. Take a lasagne sheet and place heaped tablespoons of the mixture along one long edge. Roll up and arrange in a single layer in a greased 2 litre (70 fl oz/8 cup) shallow ovenproof dish. Repeat with the remaining mixture and lasagne sheets. Pour on the reserved mushroom cooking liquid then pour on the pasta sauce. Sprinkle with mozzarella cheese and bake for 25 minutes, or until golden and bubbling.

NUTRITION PER SERVE
Protein 33 g; Fat 30 g; Carbohydrate 38 g; Dietary Fibre 6 g; Cholesterol 90 mg; 2290 kJ (545 Cal)

Pumpkin, basil and ricotta lasagne

PREPARATION TIME: 20 MINUTES | TOTAL COOKING TIME: 1 HOUR 25 MINUTES | SERVES 4

650 g (1 lb 7 oz) pumpkin (winter squash)
2 tablespoons olive oil
500 g (1 lb 2 oz/2 cups) ricotta cheese
60 g (2¼ oz/⅓ cup) pine nuts, toasted
1 very large handful basil
2 garlic cloves, crushed
30 g (1 oz/⅓ cup) grated parmesan cheese
125 g (4½ oz) fresh lasagne sheets
185 g (6½ oz/1¼ cups) grated mozzarella
   cheese

1 Preheat the oven to 180°C (350°F/Gas 4). Lightly grease a baking tray. Cut the pumpkin into thin slices and arrange in a single layer on the tray. Brush with oil and cook for 1 hour, or until softened, turning halfway through cooking.

2 Mix together the ricotta, pine nuts, basil, garlic and parmesan.

3 Brush a square 20 cm (8 inch) ovenproof dish with oil. Cook the lasagne sheets in a large saucepan of rapidly boiling water for 2–3 minutes, stirring gently. Drain well. Arrange one-third of the pasta sheets over the base of the dish. Spread with the ricotta mixture. Top with half the remaining lasagne sheets.

4 Arrange the pumpkin evenly over the pasta with as few gaps as possible. Season with salt and freshly ground black pepper and top with the final layer of pasta sheets. Sprinkle with mozzarella. Bake for 20–25 minutes, or until the cheese is golden. Leave for 10 minutes, then cut into squares.

NOTE: *If the pasta has no cooking instructions, blanch the sheets one at a time.*

Mix together the ricotta, pine nuts, basil, garlic and parmesan.

Arrange the pumpkin on top of the lasagne sheet, leaving as few gaps as possible.

NUTRITION PER SERVE
Protein 24 g; Fat 32 g; Carbohydrate 33 g; Dietary Fibre 4.5 g; Cholesterol 37 mg; 2166 kJ (517 Cal)

Pastitsio

PREPARATION TIME: 1 HOUR | TOTAL COOKING TIME: 1 HOUR 40 MINUTES | SERVES 8

2 tablespoons olive oil

4 garlic cloves, crushed

3 onions, chopped

1 kg (2 lb 4 oz) minced (ground) lamb

800 g (1 lb 12 oz) tinned chopped tomatoes

250 ml (9 fl oz/1 cup) dry red wine

250 ml (9 fl oz/1 cup) chicken stock

3 tablespoons tomato paste (concentrated purée)

2 tablespoons oregano leaves

2 bay leaves

350 g (12 oz) ziti or spaghetti

2 eggs, lightly beaten

750 g (1 lb 10 oz/3 cups) Greek-style yoghurt

3 eggs, extra, lightly beaten

200 g (7 oz) kefalotyri or manchego cheese, grated (see NOTE)

½ teaspoon ground nutmeg

50 g (1¾ oz/½ cup) grated parmesan cheese

80 g (2¾ oz/1 cup) fresh breadcrumbs

NUTRITION PER SERVE:
Protein 50 g; Fat 40 g; Carbohydrate 45 g; Dietary Fibre 5 g; Cholesterol 250 mg; 3275 kJ (780 Cal)

1 Preheat the oven to 200°C (400°F/Gas 6). To make the meat sauce, heat the oil in a large heavy-based saucepan and cook the garlic and onion over low heat for 10 minutes, or until the onion is soft and golden.

2 Add the lamb and cook over high heat until browned, stirring constantly and breaking up any lumps with a wooden spoon. Add the tomato, wine, stock, tomato paste, oregano and bay leaves. Bring to the boil, reduce the heat and simmer, covered, for 15 minutes. Remove the lid and cook for 30 minutes. Season with salt and pepper.

3 While the meat is cooking, cook the pasta in a large saucepan of rapidly boiling salted water until *al dente*. Drain well. Transfer to a bowl and stir the eggs through. Spoon into a lightly greased 4 litre (140 fl oz/16 cup) ovenproof dish. Top with the meat sauce.

4 Whisk the yoghurt, extra eggs, cheese and nutmeg in a bowl to combine and pour the mixture over the meat sauce. Sprinkle with the combined parmesan cheese and breadcrumbs. Bake for 30–35 minutes, or until the top of the pastitsio is crisp and golden. Leave for 20 minutes before slicing.

NOTE: *Kefalotyri and manchego are firm, grating cheeses. Use parmesan if they are unavailable.*

Cook the minced lamb until browned before adding the tomato, wine, stock, tomato paste and herbs.

Cook the pasta until *al dente* then mix with the eggs. Press into the dish.

Pour the mixture of yoghurt, eggs, cheese and nutmeg over the meat sauce.

Baked meatballs and pasta

PREPARATION TIME: 25 MINUTES | TOTAL COOKING TIME: 1 HOUR | SERVES 4

100 g (3½ oz) macaroni
500 g (1 lb 2 oz) minced (ground) beef
1 onion, finely chopped
2 tablespoons grated parmesan cheese
1 tablespoon chopped basil
1 egg, beaten
90 g (3¼ oz/1 cup) fresh breadcrumbs
2 tablespoons olive oil
150 g (5½ oz/1 cup) grated mozzarella cheese

SAUCE
1 onion, sliced
1 garlic clove, crushed
1 capsicum (pepper), seeded and sliced
125 g (4½ oz) button mushrooms, sliced
3 tablespoons tomato paste (concentrated
    purée)
125 ml (4 fl oz/½ cup) dry red wine

1 Cook the pasta in a large saucepan of rapidly boiling salted water until *al dente*. Drain well and return to the pan to keep warm. Mix together the minced beef, onion, parmesan, basil, egg and half the breadcrumbs. Form heaped teaspoons of the mixture into balls.

2 Heat the oil in a frying pan and cook the meatballs until well browned. Drain on paper towels. Transfer to an ovenproof dish. Preheat the oven to 180°C (350°F/Gas 4).

3 To make the sauce, add the onion and garlic to the same pan and stir over low heat until tender. Add the capsicum and mushrooms and cook for 2 minutes. Stir in the tomato paste. Add 250 ml (9 fl oz/1 cup) water and the wine and bring to the boil. Mix in the macaroni and salt and pepper. Pour over the meatballs.

4 Bake for 30–35 minutes. Sprinkle with the mozzarella and remaining breadcrumbs. Bake for another 10 minutes, or until golden.

Form heaped teaspoons of the mixture into small meatballs.

Fry the meatballs until they are well browned, then drain on paper towels.

NUTRITION PER SERVE
Protein 44 g; Fat 34 g; Carbohydrate 38 g; Dietary Fibre 4 g; Cholesterol 150 mg; 2740 kJ (650 Cal)

Pasta soufflé

PREPARATION TIME: 20 MINUTES I TOTAL COOKING TIME: 55 MINUTES I SERVES 4

2 tablespoons grated parmesan cheese
60 g (2¼ oz) salted butter
1 small onion, finely chopped
2 tablespoons plain (all-purpose) flour
500 ml (17 fl oz/2 cups) milk
125 ml (4 fl oz/½ cup) chicken stock
3 eggs, separated
125 g (4½ oz) small macaroni, cooked
210 g (7½ oz) tinned salmon, drained and
    flaked
1 tablespoon chopped parsley
grated zest of 1 lemon

1   Preheat the oven to 210°C (415°F/Gas 6–7).
Brush a round 18 cm (7 inch) soufflé dish with
oil. Coat base and sides with parmesan cheese,
shaking off the excess. Make a collar for the dish
by cutting a piece of aluminium foil or baking
paper a little longer than the dish circumference.
Fold the foil or baking paper in half lengthways
and wrap around the outside of dish so that it
extends about 5 cm (2 inches) above the rim.
Secure with string.

2   Heat the butter in a large saucepan and
cook the onion over low heat until tender.
Add the flour. Stir for 2 minutes, or until
golden. Remove from the heat and gradually
stir in the milk and stock until smooth. Return
to the heat and stir constantly until the mixture
boils and thickens. Reduce the heat and simmer
for 3 minutes. Add the egg yolks and whisk until
smooth. Add the macaroni, salmon, parsley,
lemon zest and season. Stir, transfer to a bowl
to cool.

3   Beat the egg whites in a small dry bowl
until stiff peaks form. With a metal spoon, fold
into the mixture. Spoon into the soufflé dish.
Bake for 40–45 minutes, or until well risen.
Serve immediately.

NUTRITION PER SERVE
Protein 27 g; Fat 26 g; Carbohydrate 34 g; Dietary
Fibre 2 g; Cholesterol 200 mg; 1994 kJ (476 Cal)

Make a collar for the soufflé dish by tying a strip of
foil around the outside.

Add the macaroni, salmon, parsley, lemon zest and
some salt and pepper.

Macaroni eggplant bake

PREPARATION TIME: 30 MINUTES + 20 MINUTES RESTING | TOTAL COOKING TIME: 1 HOUR | SERVES 4–6

125 g (4½ oz) macaroni

2–3 eggplants (aubergine), sliced thinly lengthways

3 tablespoons olive oil

1 onion, chopped

1 garlic clove, crushed

500 g (1 lb 2 oz) minced (ground) pork, beef or chicken

425 g (15 oz) tinned chopped tomatoes

2 tablespoons tomato paste (concentrated purée)

155 g (5½ oz/1 cup) frozen peas

150 g (5½ oz/1 cup) grated mozzarella cheese

60 g (2¼ oz/½ cup) grated cheddar cheese

1 egg, beaten

60 g (2¼ oz) grated parmesan cheese

NUTRITION PER SERVE (6)
Protein 40 g; Fat 22 g; Carbohydrate 20 g; Dietary Fibre 5 g; Cholesterol 120 mg; 1866 kJ (446 Cal)

1 Grease and line a deep 23 cm (9 inch) round spring-form cake tin. Cook the pasta in a large saucepan of rapidly boiling salted water until *al dente.* Drain well and return to the pan to keep warm. Arrange the eggplant in a large colander and sprinkle generously with salt. Leave for 20 minutes, then rinse well. Pat dry with paper towels. Heat 2 tablespoons of the oil in a frying pan and fry the eggplant in batches in a single layer until golden on each side. Add more oil as required. Drain on paper towels.

2 Add the onion and garlic to the same pan and stir over low heat until tender. Add the meat and cook until browned. Add the tomato, tomato paste, season and stir well. Bring to the boil. Reduce the heat and simmer for 15–20 minutes, then set aside.

3 Mix together the peas, macaroni, mozzarella and cheddar cheese, egg and half the parmesan.

4 Preheat the oven to 180°C (350°F/ Gas 4). Place a slice of eggplant in the centre of the tin. Arrange three-quarters of the remaining eggplant in an overlapping pattern to completely cover the base and side of the tin. Sprinkle with half the remaining parmesan.

5 Combine the meat with the macaroni mixture. Spoon the filling into the eggplant shell, packing down well. Arrange the remaining eggplant slices, overlapping, over the filling. Sprinkle with the parmesan. Bake for 25–30 minutes, or until golden. Leave for 5 minutes, then out onto a serving plate.

Salt the eggplant to draw out any bitterness, then fry in a single layer until golden.

Line the base and side of the tin with the eggplant slices to make a shell.

Leave the bake to rest for 5 minutes so that it firms up before turning out.

Pasta salads

Warm pesto and prawn salad

PREPARATION TIME: 15 MINUTES I TOTAL COOKING TIME: 20 MINUTES I SERVES 4

PESTO
2 garlic cloves, crushed
1 teaspoon salt
40 g (1½ oz/¼ cup) pine nuts, toasted
2 very large handfuls basil
60 g (2¼ oz) grated parmesan cheese
3 tablespoons extra virgin olive oil

500 g (1 lb 2 oz) pasta
150 g (5½ oz) jar capers in brine
3 tablespoons olive oil
2 tablespoons extra virgin olive oil
2 garlic cloves, chopped
2 tomatoes, seeded and diced
150 g (5½ oz) asparagus spears trimmed,
    halved and blanched
2 tablespoons balsamic vinegar
150 g (5½ oz) rocket (arugula)
20 cooked prawns (shrimp), peeled, tails
    intact
shaved parmesan cheese, for serving

1   For the pesto, blend the garlic, salt, pine nuts, basil leaves and parmesan cheese in a food processor or blender until thoroughly combined. With the motor running, add the oil in a thin steady stream and process until the pesto is smooth.

2   Cook the pasta in a large saucepan of rapidly boiling salted water until *al dente*. Drain well, transfer to a large bowl and toss the pesto through.

3   Pat the drained capers dry with paper towels, then heat the olive oil in a frying pan and fry the capers for 4–5 minutes, stirring occasionally, until crisp. Drain on paper towels.

4   Heat the extra virgin olive oil in a deep frying pan over medium heat and add the garlic, tomato and asparagus. Toss continuously for 1–2 minutes, or until warmed through. Stir in the balsamic vinegar.

5   When the pasta is just warm, not hot (or it will wilt the rocket), toss the tomato mixture, rocket and prawns through it and season with salt and pepper, to taste. Serve sprinkled with capers and shaved parmesan (if desired).

Fry the drained capers in the hot oil, stirring occasionally, until crisp.

NUTRITION PER SERVE
Protein 42 g; Fat 52 g; Carbohydrate 92 g; Dietary Fibre 10 g; Cholesterol 163 mg; 4195 kJ (1000 Cal)

Salami pasta salad

PREPARATION TIME: 20 MINUTES | TOTAL COOKING TIME: 15 MINUTES | SERVES 8

1 red capsicum (pepper), cut into strips
1 green capsicum (pepper), cut into strips
4 celery stalks, sliced
1 fennel bulb, trimmed and sliced
1 red onion, sliced
200 g (7 oz) salami, thickly sliced and then cut into strips
1 large handful chopped flat-leaf (Italian) parsley
300 g (10½ oz) fettuccine

DRESSING
125 ml (4 fl oz/½ cup) olive oil
3 tablespoons lemon juice
2½ tablespoons dijon mustard
1 teaspoon sugar
1 garlic clove, crushed

1 Mix together the capsicum, celery, fennel, onion, salami and parsley in a large bowl.

2 Cook the pasta in a large saucepan of rapidly boiling salted water until *al dente*. Drain well and rinse under cold water. Add to the bowl and toss with the vegetables and salami.

3 To make the dressing, combine the olive oil, lemon juice, mustard, sugar and crushed garlic and season to taste. Pour over the pasta salad and toss well.

Use a sharp knife to halve the fennel and then cut into slices.

Cut the salami into strips and add to the vegetables along with the chopped parsley.

NUTRITION PER SERVE
Protein 10 g; Fat 25 g; Carbohydrate 30 g; Dietary Fibre 2.5 g; Cholesterol 26 mg; 1599 kJ (380 Cal)

Grilled capsicum and anchovy salad

PREPARATION TIME: 15 MINUTES | TOTAL COOKING TIME: 25 MINUTES | SERVES 4–6

500 g (1 lb 2 oz) penne or spiral pasta
2 large red capsicums (peppers)
1 small red onion, finely chopped
2 large handfuls flat-leaf (Italian) parsley
    leaves
2 anchovies, whole or chopped
3 tablespoons olive oil
2 tablespoons lemon juice

1   Cook the pasta in a large saucepan of rapidly boiling salted water until *al dente*. Drain and rinse under cold water.

2   Cut the capsicum into large pieces, removing the seeds and membrane. Place skin side up under a hot grill (broiler) and cook for 8 minutes, or until the skin is blistered and black. Cool in a plastic bag, then peel away the skin and cut the flesh into thin strips.

3   Toss together the pasta, capsicum, onion, parsley, anchovies, oil, lemon juice and season. Serve immediately.

HINT: *The capsicum can be peeled a day in advance, covered well and then refrigerated. Removing the skin in this way results in a much sweeter taste.*

NUTRITION PER SERVE (6)
Protein 11 g; Fat 11 g; Carbohydrate 62 g; Dietary Fibre 7 g; Cholesterol 0 mg; 1640 kJ (400 Cal)

Cut the red onion in half and then use a sharp knife to finely chop.

Remove the seeds and membrane from the capsicum before grilling (broiling).

Put all the ingredients in a large bowl and toss together well.

Mediterranean pasta salad with black olive dressing

PREPARATION TIME: 30 MINUTES | TOTAL COOKING TIME: 25 MINUTES | SERVES 4

250 g (9 oz) spiral pasta
1 red capsicum (pepper)
1 yellow or green capsicum (pepper)
1 tablespoon sunflower oil
2 tablespoons olive oil
2 garlic cloves, crushed
1 eggplant (aubergine), cubed
2 zucchini (courgettes), thickly sliced
2 large ripe tomatoes, peeled, seeded and
　　chopped (see NOTE)
1 handful chopped flat-leaf (Italian) parsley
150 g (5½ oz/1 cup) crumbled feta cheese

BLACK OLIVE DRESSING
6 large marinated black olives, pitted
125 ml (4 fl oz/½ cup) olive oil
2 tablespoons balsamic vinegar

1　Cook the pasta in a large saucepan of rapidly boiling salted water until *al dente*. Drain well, spread in a single layer on a baking tray to dry, then refrigerate, uncovered, until chilled.

2　Cut the capsicum into large pieces, removing the seeds and membrane. Place, skin side up, under a hot grill (broiler) until the skin blackens and blisters. Leave to cool in a plastic bag, then peel away the skin. Slice the flesh into thick strips.

3　Heat the sunflower and olive oil in a frying pan. Add the garlic and eggplant and fry quickly, tossing, until lightly browned. Remove from the heat and place in a large bowl. Steam the zucchini for 1–2 minutes, or until just tender. Rinse under cold water, drain and add to the eggplant.

4　To make the dressing, process the olives in a food processor until finely chopped. Gradually add the olive oil, processing until thoroughly combined after each addition. Add the vinegar, season and process to combine.

5　Combine the pasta, capsicum, eggplant, zucchini, tomato, parsley and 1 teaspoon pepper in a large bowl. Top with the feta and drizzle with the dressing.

NOTE: *To peel tomatoes, score a cross in the base of each tomato. Leave in a pan of boiling water for 1 minute, then plunge into cold water. Peel the skin away from the cross. To remove the seeds, cut the tomato in half and scoop out the seeds with a teaspoon.*

NUTRITION PER SERVE
Protein 15 g; Fat 55 g; Carbohydrate 50 g; Dietary Fibre 8 g; Cholesterol 25 mg; 3220 kJ (765 Cal)

Drain the cooked pasta and spread on a tray to dry and cool.

Remove the seeds and white membrane from the capsicums and cut into large pieces.

Fry the garlic and cubed eggplant quickly until it is lightly browned.

Farfalle salad with sun-dried tomatoes and spinach

PREPARATION TIME: 20 MINUTES | TOTAL COOKING TIME: 15 MINUTES | SERVES 4–6

500 g (1 lb 2 oz) farfalle or spiral pasta
3 spring onions (scallions)
60 g (2¼ oz) sun-dried tomatoes, cut into
  strips
500 g (1 lb 2 oz) English spinach, shredded
50 g (1¾ oz/⅓ cup) pine nuts, toasted
1 tablespoon chopped oregano

DRESSING
3 tablespoons olive oil
1 teaspoon chopped chilli
1 garlic clove, crushed

1   Cook the pasta in a large saucepan of rapidly boiling salted water until *al dente.* Drain well and rinse under cold water. Transfer to a large salad bowl. Trim the spring onions and chop finely. Add to the pasta with the tomato, spinach, pine nuts and oregano.

2   To make the dressing, put the oil, chilli and garlic in a small screw-top jar and season to taste. Shake well.

3   Pour the dressing over the salad, toss well and serve immediately.

NUTRITION PER SERVE (6)
Protein 12 g; Fat 8 g; Carbohydrate 60 g; Dietary Fibre 6 g; Cholesterol 0 mg; 1490 kJ (357 Cal)

Pour the dressing over the salad and then toss together before serving.

Warm sweet potato, walnut and pasta salad

PREPARATION TIME: 15 MINUTES | TOTAL COOKING TIME: 30 MINUTES | SERVES 4

800 g (1 lb 12 oz) orange sweet potato, cut into small cubes
150 ml (5 fl oz) olive oil
125 g (4½ oz/1 cup) walnut pieces
350 g (12 oz) pasta
150 g (5½ oz) triple-cream, mould-ripened cheese
2 garlic cloves, crushed
2 teaspoons lemon juice
½ teaspoon sugar
100 g (3½ oz) rocket (arugula)

1 Preheat the oven to 200°C (400°F/Gas 6). Toss the orange sweet potato in 2 tablespoons of the oil and place in a single layer on a baking tray lined with baking paper. Season with salt and pepper. Cook, turning halfway through, for 30 minutes, or until golden and cooked through. Spread the walnuts onto a separate baking tray and add to the oven for the last 10 minutes, or until crisp and golden.

2 Meanwhile, cook the pasta in a large saucepan of rapidly boiling salted water until *al dente*. Drain well and return to the pan to keep warm. Remove the rind from one-third of the cheese and cut the rest into cubes. Finely chop 2 tablespoons of the toasted walnuts and place in a screw-top jar with the garlic, lemon juice, sugar, remaining oil and rindless cheese and season. Shake the jar until well combined. You may need to break the cheese up with a fork to help mix it through if it is too firm.

3 Toss the pasta, sweet potato, rocket, cubed cheese and remaining walnuts in a bowl, drizzle with the dressing and toss together. Divide among four serving bowls and season to taste with salt and freshly ground black pepper.

Spread the walnuts on a baking tray and toast for 10 minutes.

Remove the rind from one-third of the cheese and cut the rest into cubes.

NUTRITION PER SERVE
Protein 27 g; Fat 69 g; Carbohydrate 92 g; Dietary Fibre 11 g; Cholesterol 38 mg; 4570 kJ (1090 Cal)

Pasta, bean salad with cumin and coriander dressing

PREPARATION TIME: 25 MINUTES | TOTAL COOKING TIME: 15 MINUTES | SERVES 6

300 g (10½ oz) fusilli (or other spiral pasta)

2 tablespoons sunflower oil

1 leek, sliced

1 red capsicum (pepper), seeded and diced

125 g (4½ oz) finely shredded English spinach

150 g (5½ oz) button mushrooms, halved

300 g (10½ oz) tinned red kidney beans, drained and rinsed

300 g (10½ oz) tinned butter beans, drained and rinsed

2 tablespoons snipped chives

60 g (2¼ oz) sunflower seeds, toasted

CUMIN AND CORIANDER DRESSING

2 garlic cloves, crushed

½ teaspoon ground cumin

½ teaspoon ground coriander

2 tablespoons cider vinegar

125 ml (4 fl oz/½ cup) olive oil

1 Cook the pasta in a large saucepan of rapidly boiling salted water until *al dente.* Drain well.

2 Heat the oil in a large saucepan, add the leek and capsicum and stir-fry over medium heat for 2–3 minutes. Add the spinach and mushrooms and toss together for about 1 minute, or until the spinach just wilts.

3 To make the dressing, mix the garlic, cumin, coriander and vinegar together. Gradually add the olive oil and whisk to combine.

4 Toss together the pasta, vegetables, beans, chives and ½ teaspoon of freshly ground black pepper. Toss with the dressing and sprinkle with the sunflower seeds to serve.

NUTRITION PER SERVE
Protein 15 g; Fat 30 g; Carbohydrate 45 g; Dietary Fibre 10 g; Cholesterol 0 mg; 2215 kJ (525 Cal)

Add the spinach and mushrooms to the leek and capsicum and cook until the spinach wilts.

Gradually whisk the oil into the combined garlic, cumin, coriander and vinegar.

Pour the dressing into the salad and toss gently to mix through.

Pesto beef salad

PREPARATION TIME: 30 MINUTES | TOTAL COOKING TIME: 25 MINUTES | SERVES 4

100 g (3½ oz) button mushrooms
1 large yellow capsicum (pepper)
1 large red capsicum (pepper)
cooking oil spray
100 g (3½ oz) lean fillet steak
125 g (4½ oz/1½ cups) penne

PESTO
2 large handfuls basil leaves
2 garlic cloves, chopped
2 tablespoons pepitas (pumpkin seeds)
1 tablespoon olive oil
2 tablespoons orange juice
1 tablespoon lemon juice

1   Cut the mushrooms into quarters. Cut the capsicums into quarters, discarding the seeds and membrane. Grill (broil) the capsicum, skin side up, until the skins blacken and blister. Cool under a damp tea towel (dish towel), then peel and dice the flesh.

2   Spray a non-stick frying pan with oil and cook the steak over high heat for 3–4 minutes on each side. Remove and leave for 5 minutes before cutting into thin slices. Season with a little salt.

3   To make the pesto, finely chop the basil leaves, garlic and pepitas in a food processor. With the motor running, add the oil, orange and lemon juice. Season well.

4   Meanwhile, cook the pasta in a large saucepan of rapidly boiling salted water until *al dente*. Drain well and toss with the pesto in a large bowl.

5   Add the capsicum pieces, steak slices and mushroom quarters to the penne and toss to distribute evenly. Serve immediately.

Cook the steak in a non-stick frying pan until it is medium-rare.

Add the oil as well as the orange and lemon juice in a thin stream.

NUTRITION PER SERVE
Protein 15 g; Fat 10 g; Carbohydrate 30 g; Dietary Fibre 4 g; Cholesterol 15 mg; 1330 kJ (270 Cal)

Spaghetti tomato salad

PREPARATION TIME: 25 MINUTES | TOTAL COOKING TIME: 15 MINUTES | SERVES 4–6

500 g (1 lb 2 oz) spaghetti
1 very large handful basil leaves
250 g (9 oz) cherry tomatoes, halved
1 garlic clove, crushed
60 g (2¼ oz/½ cup) chopped black olives
3 tablespoons olive oil
1 tablespoon balsamic vinegar
60 g (2¼ oz/½ cup) grated parmesan cheese

1 Cook the pasta in a large saucepan of rapidly boiling salted water until *al dente*. Drain well and rinse under cold water. Using a sharp knife, chop the basil leaves into fine strips.

2 Mix together the basil, tomato, garlic, olives, oil and vinegar. Leave for 15 minutes. Toss with the pasta.

3 Add the parmesan and season with salt and pepper. Toss well to serve.

NUTRITION PER SERVE (6)
Protein 14 g; Fat 15 g; Carbohydrate 65 g; Dietary Fibre 14 g; Cholesterol 10 mg; 1866 kJ (446 Cal)

Chop the basil leaves just before you are ready to use them as the cut edges turn black.

Mix together the basil, tomato, garlic, olives, oil and vinegar and leave to stand.

After tossing the pasta salad, add the parmesan and salt and pepper then toss again.

Chicken and pasta salad

PREPARATION TIME: 30 MINUTES | TOTAL COOKING TIME: 25 MINUTES | SERVES 4

250 g (9 oz) boneless, skinless chicken
  breasts
375 ml (13 fl oz/1½ cups) chicken stock
350 g (12 oz) spiral pasta
150 g (5½ oz) asparagus spears, cut into short
  lengths
150 g (5½ oz) gruyère cheese, grated
2 spring onions (scallions), finely sliced

DRESSING
3 tablespoons olive oil
3 tablespoons lemon juice
½ teaspoon sugar

1 Put the chicken and stock in a frying pan. Bring to the boil, reduce the heat and poach gently, turning regularly, for 8 minutes, or until tender. Remove, cool and slice thinly.

2 Cook the pasta in a large saucepan of rapidly boiling salted water until *al dente*. Drain well and cool.

3 Cook the asparagus in boiling water for 2 minutes. Drain and place in a bowl of iced water. Drain again. Combine with the chicken, pasta and cheese in a large bowl.

4 To make the dressing, whisk the ingredients together. Season with salt and pepper. Add to the salad and toss well. Transfer to a serving bowl and scatter with the spring onions.

Chop the asparagus, grate the cheese and finely slice the spring onion.

Cook the asparagus in a small saucepan of boiling water for 2 minutes.

NUTRITION PER SERVE
Protein 40 g; Fat 30 g; Carbohydrate 60 g; Dietary Fibre 5 g; Cholesterol 70 mg; 2785 kJ (665 Cal)

Index

Index

Published in 2008 by Murdoch Books Pty Limited.

Murdoch Books Australia
Pier 8/9, 23 Hickson Road
Millers Point NSW 2000
Phone: + 61 (0) 2 8220 2000
Fax: + 61 (0) 2 8220 2558
www.murdochbooks.com.au

Murdoch Books UK Limited
Erico House, 6th Floor
93–99 Upper Richmond Road
Putney, London SW15 2TG
Phone: + 44 (0) 20 8785 5995
Fax: + 44 (0) 20 8785 5985
www.murdochbooks.co.uk

Chief Executive: Juliet Rogers
Publishing Director: Kay Scarlett

Project manager: Paul O'Beirne
Editor: Vicky Fisher
Design concept: Heather Menzies
Design: Heather Menzies and Jacqueline Richards
Photographer: Alan Benson
Stylist: Mary Harris
Food preparation: Joanne Glynn
Introduction text: Leanne Kitchen
Production: Monique Layt

National Library of Australia Cataloguing-in-Publication Data
Homestyle Pasta. Includes index.
ISBN 978 1 74196 167 6 (pbk.).
1. Cookery (pasta). I. Title. 641.822

A catalogue record for this book is available from the British Library.

Colour separation by Splitting Image in Clayton, Victoria, Australia.
Printed by i-Book Printing Ltd. in 2008. PRINTED IN CHINA.

IMPORTANT: Those who might be at risk from the effects of salmonella poisoning
(the elderly, pregnant women, young children and those suffering from immune deficiency diseases)
should consult their doctor with any concerns about eating raw eggs.

CONVERSION GUIDE: You may find cooking times vary depending on the oven
you are using. For fan-forced ovens, as a general rule, set the oven temperature
to 20°C (35°F) lower than indicated in the recipe.